# INTO
# LIBERTY

The Basics of Christianity and
New Testament Church Life

## George Alexander

# INTO LIBERTY

The Basics of Christianity and
New Testament Church Life

## George Alexander

# INTO LIBERTY

*The Basics of Christianity and New Testament Church Life*

by George Alexander

ISBN 978-0-9955601-0-9

Unless otherwise stated, all Scripture references are from the *Holy Bible: New International Version* (NIV), copyright © 1973, 1978, 1984 by the International Bible Society.  Used by permission of Hodder & Stoughton.

Artios Publishing
Liberty Centre
Pitreavie Way
Pitreavie Business Park
Dunfermline
Fife KY11 8QS
www.artios.org
mail@artios.org

# Dedication

This book is dedicated in a general sense to all the people and leaders of Liberty Church of Dunfermline, Scotland. Thank you for your warmth and welcome, from my very first meeting in the summer of 1980, through my official "joining" in early 1983, to my taking over as pastor in July 1985. Thank you also for your faithfulness, patience and willingness to follow, through my years of pastoring, through my move into more of a teaching ministry, and on to the present day. I believe along with you that, for Liberty Church, the best is yet to come.

This book is dedicated more specifically to Jon and Fiona Farrimond, the present pastors of Liberty Church. Thank you for your friendship. In it, I look forward to continuing to work fruitfully together. Your openness is refreshing, your emphasis is engaging, your style is enthusing. Your hands are safe hands. In the light of that, may the Lord increase and multiply the numbers of new people He sends *Into Liberty*.

George Alexander
August 2016

# Contents

# Introduction

What are the basics of Christianity? Where do we start in talking about Jesus Christ, walking in relationship with Him, and living as part of the Church? Should we focus only on the truths of personal salvation and discipleship? Or are there also areas of interaction with one another that we must include?

How does a local church add new members? What if these new people have transferred into the area from a previous church, and their expectations, based on that previous experience, are different from the reality of life in the new church? How do we explain our style and values and help these new people to connect?

These are the kinds of questions that local churches have asked and debated over the years. The usual outworking is to put together a course, sometimes called a membership course and sometimes a commitment course, that seeks to cover the basics and explain "how things work here".

The material of this book began life as such a course. It was originally written as the introductory course for Liberty Church in Dunfermline, Scotland. Liberty Church has an unusual history for a Scottish church in that it was founded by a small team of missionaries sent for the purpose from a church in Pensacola, Florida in 1979. The goal of the missionaries was to raise up local leadership, and hand the Church over to them. And so it was that my wife and I took over the pastorate of the Church in 1985. I pastored Liberty Church for a number of years, in the process trying out various kinds of "membership courses". Although the current pastor Jon Farrimond is the second after me, I am still based in Liberty Church and a part of the leadership. One of my responsibilities was to put together the current course, which has now become this book.

Since the Church is called Liberty Church, the title "Into Liberty" seems an appropriate one. It is however appropriate in another sense. In John 8, Jesus said to the Jews who had believed in Him:

*If you hold to my teaching you are really my disciples.*
*Then you will know the truth, and the truth will set you*
*free.* John 8:31,32

In other words, the truth will move you into liberty.

Then a few verses later, He says, *"If the Son sets you free, you will be free indeed."* (John 8:36)

It is my hope and prayer that through these chapters many will be helped to experience that freedom, and truly moved *into liberty*.

# ONE

# First Things First: What About The Bible?

**KEY VERSE:** All Scripture is God-breathed and is useful for teaching, rebuking, correcting and training in righteousness, so that the man of God may be thoroughly equipped for every good work.

2 Timothy 3:16,17

*It's not my opinion that matters, Lord, but what you say in your Word.*

Colin Urquhart

## Setting the scene

The Bible is really a library, a collection of sixty-six books (thirty-nine Old Testament, twenty-seven New) written by some forty human authors.  Yet it all hangs together with absolute consistency, because behind the scenes of human authorship, it's authored by God.

It's been called the "Manufacturer's Handbook for Living".  It's not just that we've got hold of it, but rather that it was written for our benefit.  God wanted us to have it.

How we view the Bible is *the central thing* that separates and distinguishes church from church.  If we ever depart from the standard of the Bible, we enter into bondage in that area—see John 8:31,32.

The Bible is in two parts: the Old Testament and the New Testament.  Both these parts have been given a referencing system of chapters and verses.  This happened long after they were written, and is not "inspired" in the way that the text is.  However it is very useful in order to find and refer to the various verses.

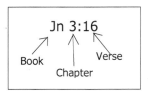

A Bible reference usually starts with an abbreviation of the book name, for example *Gen* for Genesis or *Jn* for John.  Then there are two numbers separated by a colon.  The number before the colon is the chapter, and the numbers after it refer to the verses.  For instance, the reference *Jn 3:16* would mean John's gospel, chapter 3 and verse 16.

The Old Testament was originally written, for the most part, in Hebrew, and the New Testament in Greek.  So the Bibles we have are translations from these languages.  We have no shortage of different translations in our own language!  These have different purposes in terms of their translation philosophy.  Some focus on word-for-word accuracy, others on communicating the meaning, and still others on readability and ease of understanding.  There are several "general purpose" translations that strike a good balance.

The Old Testament starts with the five books of *the Law*, namely *Genesis*, *Exodus*, *Leviticus*, *Numbers* and *Deuteronomy*. Sometimes referred to as *the Pentateuch*, these books tell the earlier part of the story, and contain the commandments, including the Ten Commandments.  They are also called *the books of Moses*, who is considered to be the writer of most of them.

Next in our English Bibles comes *the History*, from *Joshua* to *Esther*. This tells the continuing story of the people of God, their Kings' period, the divided monarchy, and their exile and partial return.  There are many important lessons for us here.

Then there is the *Wisdom* or *Poetry* section, from *Job* to *Song of Solomon*. These books are well beloved of Bible readers, and contain many favourite verses. There we find comfort and strength, praise and worship, a breadth of emotions, practical wisdom—in a word, inspiration.

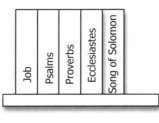

Finally in the Old Testament come *the Prophets*, from *Isaiah* to *Malachi*. These are often divided into two groups called the *Major Prophets* and the *Minor Prophets*, although this distinction has to do with the *length* of the books, not their *importance*.

Then comes the *New Testament*, starting with the *Matthew, Mark, Luke,* and *John*. These are called *the Gospels*, and tell the story and events of the life of Jesus on earth, from before His birth right through until after His resurrection from the dead. His *teaching* of course figures prominently.

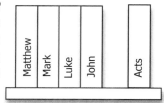

The book of *Acts* then continues the story, telling the history of the first thirty years or so of the church and its spread in Judea and Samaria, and on into Asia (we would say Asia Minor) and Europe.

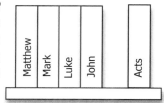

From *Romans* to *Jude* are the *Letters* or *Epistles*. There are twenty-one of these, most of them written by the Apostle Paul. They are letters to churches and individuals, often written in response to situations and questions, or to correct problems and misunderstandings. They are highly important to us today, as we follow Jesus with sound doctrine.

Finally, in a category of its own, there is *Revelation*. This is a prophetic book, written in symbolic language. It is somewhat controversial in that it is understood and applied very differently by different sections of the church. However, its message is one of encouragement.

> *"The truly wise man is he who believes the Bible against the opinions of any man. If the Bible says one thing and any body of men says another, the wise man will decide, 'This book is the Word of Him who cannot lie.'"*
>
> R.A. Torrey

**How we view the Bible**

The Bible is for us the objective standard of revelation and practice. It's the standard in *hearing from God*. Anything we think we hear God say must line up with the Bible and be subject to it, otherwise God did not really say it. He doesn't contradict Himself.

One of the ways that God speaks today is through *prophecy*, where He still speaks to and through people. But the Bible always has greater weight—it's on a different plane. All supposed prophetic utterance must align with and be subject to the Bible. If not, it didn't come from God.

It's also the standard in *living*. We *live by the Word*. Quoting from the Old Testament, Jesus said, *"Man does not live on bread alone, but on every word that comes from the mouth of God."* (Matthew 4:4) In the Psalms, we find:

> *Your word is a lamp to my feet and a light for my path.*
> Psalm 119:105
> *Direct my footsteps according to your word.*
> Psalm 119:133

In this regard, our basic response to the Bible is one of *obedience.*

The Bible is worth our *reading*, *study* and *meditation*. Herrick Johnson, a preacher from a former generation, said:

> *"If God is a reality, and the soul is a reality, and you are an immortal being, what are you doing with your Bible shut?"*

When it comes to reading, study and meditation, you have to start somewhere! As regards reading, a good place to start is one of the Gospels, perhaps John or Mark. Make sure you have a good modern translation. Many people find Bible-reading notes helpful, or some kind of Bible-reading plan. Some plans give a few verses to read every day; others give three to five chapters, and following them means we read the whole Bible in a year.

Studying takes us deeper, perhaps focusing on a particular passage, character or topic. There are many tools available that can help us.

Meditation in a biblical sense is not about chanting, sitting in a particular position, or emptying the mind! On the contrary, it's about filling the mind with thoughts from the Bible. Usually, this consists of taking a few verses and repeatedly *chewing them over* in the mind and holding them in the heart.   A good way to begin this is to *memorise* the verse or verses in question.

In Ephesians, part of the picture of the armour of God that enables us to stand is *the sword of the Spirit, which is the word of God* (see Eph 6:10-18).   Certain Bible verses can be very useful as "weapons" to defend ourselves against temptation or attacks of the enemy. *Memorising* these verses is like taking them into our personal arsenal, and can be very powerful in its effects.

## KEY TRUTH:

We believe the Bible to be God's word.  It is entirely trustworthy, and is our supreme authority in all matters of faith and conduct.  It will produce faith within us, and in that faith we may overcome the challenges of life.

8    Into Liberty

# TWO

# New Life For Old

**KEY VERSE:** *We were therefore buried with Him through baptism into death in order that, just as Christ was raised from the dead through the glory of the Father, we too may live a new life.*

Romans 6:4

**KEY TRUTH:** Jesus Christ is the Son of God. He is also God the Son. He is fully God and fully man. He was conceived of the Holy Spirit, born of the Virgin Mary, and lived a perfect, sinless life. His death provided full payment for all our sins. He physically rose from the dead. He ascended into heaven and is currently interceding for us. He will one day return to the earth as Lord and Judge. As Lord of heaven and earth, He demands and deserves our worship and obedience.

We've all heard a version of the story of someone who has lost his way stopping to ask a local person for directions, only to be told: "If I was trying to get to *there*, I wouldn't start from here!" But the thing is, in order to make any progress we *have* to start from here.

The first question to ask then is: Where is here? Where are we? What's the position? What situation are we in?

In the beginning, God created everything, including mankind (see Genesis 1, especially verses 1, 26 and 27). Sadly, man disobeyed and fell in to sin. (We call this the "Fall", and we find the detail in Genesis 3:1-24.) As a result, men and women can be pictured as being separated from God by a great gulf or chasm. This gulf is caused by *sin*. Despite his best attempts, nothing man can do can bridge this gulf. We need someone to rescue us from the wrong side of the chasm, someone to bring us back and reconcile us to God. All people need a Saviour.

## How can man be reconciled to God?

The work is already done. God has taken the initiative and has reconciled us in Jesus Christ. Look at these verses:

*All this is from God, who reconciled us to himself through Christ ...*                                                    2 Corinthians 5:18

*For God was pleased to have all his fullness dwell in him, and through him to reconcile to himself all things, whether things on earth or things in heaven, by making peace through his blood, shed on the cross.*
Colossians 1:19,20

More detail on what Jesus has done can be seen in the following verses:

He saved us.

*For the Son of Man came to seek and to save what was lost.*                                                    Luke 19:10

He took away our sins.

*But you know that he appeared so that he might take away our sins.  And in him is no sin.*           1 John 3:5

He destroyed the devil's works.

*The reason the Son of God appeared was to destroy the devil's work.*                                                    1 John 3:8b

He made full payment for sin.

*But he was pierced for our transgressions, he was crushed for our iniquities; the punishment that brought us peace was upon him, and by his wounds we are healed.*
Isaiah 53:5

He made atonement for us.

*... that God was reconciling the world to himself in Christ, not counting men's sins against them. And he has committed to us the message of reconciliation.  We are therefore Christ's ambassadors, as though God were making his appeal through us.  We implore you on Christ's behalf:  Be reconciled to God.  God made him who had no sin to be sin for us, so that in him we might become the righteousness of God.*   2 Corinthians 5:19-21

To understand the word "atonement", it may help to break it up into its parts.  The atonement is the *at-one-ment*.  And how was this accomplished?  Through the cross:

*For he himself is our peace, who has made the two one and has destroyed the barrier, the dividing wall of hostility, by abolishing in his flesh the law with its commandments and regulations. His purpose was to create in himself one new man out of the two, thus making peace, and in this one body to reconcile both of them to God through the cross, by which he put to death their hostility. He came and preached peace to you who were far away and peace to those who were near. For through him we both have access to the Father by one Spirit.*                                        Ephesians 2:14-18

Something of an exchange took place, a switch.

*We all, like sheep, have gone astray, each of us has turned to his own way; and the Lord has laid on him the iniquity of us all.*                                        Isaiah 53:6

*God made him who had no sin to be sin for us, so that in him we might become the righteousness of God.*
                                        2 Corinthians 5:21

Put simply, He got what we deserved (death) so we could get what He deserved (full life).

So for us as believers in Jesus, there is *old* life and *new* life. Our old life *ends* in Him, and our new life *begins* in Him.

*Therefore, if anyone is in Christ, he is a new creation; the old has gone, the new has come!*         2 Corinthians 5:17

## How do we respond?

In Mark's Gospel, Jesus gave the answer: *"The time has come. The kingdom of God is near. Repent and believe the good news!"* (Mark 1:15). There are two parts to consider: first, repent; secondly, believe the good news.

What is *repentance*? It's a much-misunderstood concept; and that's not really surprising, because the meaning of the English word sets us off in the wrong direction. "Repent" is probably not the best English word to translate the meaning from the original languages, but it's the word that's been used for so long that we're stuck with it! The English word has to do with regret and sorrow, but the underlying biblical idea is not to do with this. Godly sorrow can *lead* to repentance (2 Corinthians 7:10), but it's not the same thing.

Biblically speaking, repentance is not being sorry.    Neither is it promising not to do it again, nor determining to try harder. Repentance is "changed thinking".    It's thinking differently afterwards from the way we thought before, and may manifest itself as a decision.    From the Old Testament, we add the moral perspective of turning from a previous way to a new way, what's been called, "the 'about-face' of a new commitment."

What is *believing*?    "Believe" translates the verb that comes from "faith", since the word "faith" does not exist as a verb in normal English.    So the instruction "repent and believe" means that our response is *repentance* and *faith*.

We're discussing the *initiation* of the Christian life, and closely associated with it is the matter of baptism in water, which we'll go on to discuss now.

### The command of water baptism

On the day of Pentecost, Peter preached to the assembled crowd, who were cut to the heart and responded with the question, "Brothers, what shall we do?"  Peter's answer began, *"Repent and be baptised, every one of you."*  (See Acts 2:37,38.)  This is certainly more of a command than a suggestion.    Similarly in the Great Commission (Matthew 28:18-20), we have in the form of an imperative, *"baptising them in the name of the Father and of the Son and of the Holy Spirit."*  When Peter went to the house of Cornelius, he ordered that they be baptised (Acts 10:48).    Baptism is a command.

But a command to do *what?*  What does it *mean?*  The underlying word means "immerse" or "submerge".    It's sometimes used of dyeing cloth.  Unfortunately, the meaning tends to be hidden because it has become a technical term that we have transliterated into English rather than translating.  If we had the courage to translate the word, it would keep the meaning rather more clear.

Note also that Jesus taught by example in this area, since He was baptised (i.e. immersed) in the Jordan by John the Baptist (or John the Immerser).

More than simply being a command, it seems that baptism is specifically a command for *believers.*  Several Scriptures can be referenced; but very straightforwardly, it says first repent then be baptised.  This is potentially a very controversial area, since a large section of the church now holds to infant baptism, in which case there is clearly no evidence that the person being baptised is a believer!  In infant baptism the *command* aspect is seen as the obedience as believers of the *parents*, resulting in their child being baptised.  But is this a practice that the New Testament actually teaches, or is it a longstanding adaptation of man in church history?  A fair question to ask would be: Can "baptism" be valid if it happened before the person concerned repented and believed?  We take the view here that this question must be answered in all good conscience.

If baptism in water is indeed a command and therefore a matter of obedience, it must follow that *not* to be baptised in water is disobedience.

### The understanding of water baptism

They may be familiar, but read again these words from Romans chapter 6:

*²We died to sin; how can we live in it any longer?  ³Or don't you know that all of us who were baptised into Christ Jesus were baptised into his death?  ⁴We were therefore buried with him through baptism into death in order that, just as Christ was raised from the dead to the glory of the Father, we too may live a new life.*

*⁵If we have been united with him like this in his death, we will certainly also be united with him in his resurrection.  ⁶For we know that our old self was crucified with him so that the body of sin might be done away with, that we should no longer be slaves to sin—⁷because anyone who has died has been freed from sin.*

*⁸Now if we died with Christ, we believe that we will also live with him.  ⁹For we know that since Christ was raised from the dead, he cannot die again; death no longer has mastery over him.  ¹⁰The death he died, he died to sin once for all; but the life he lives, he lives to God.  ¹¹In the same way, count yourselves dead to sin but alive to God in Christ Jesus.*                         Romans 6:2-11

They speak of *union* (sometimes called *oneness* or *identification*) with Christ in His death, burial and resurrection.

Fundamentally, water baptism is the burial of the old man or woman, the old nature, the old self. That self is dead in Christ, and baptism is the burial. As we come up from the waters of baptism, the symbolism is of being raised with Christ in a new nature, as a new

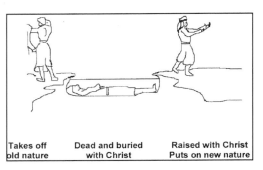

Takes off old nature    Dead and buried with Christ    Raised with Christ Puts on new nature

creation in Christ Jesus. It's an act of finality. According to 1 Corinthians 10, the Exodus is a picture of this reality. Crossing through the Red Sea, the sea closed behind them, which meant two things for the Israelites. First, they could not go back. Secondly, the Egyptians could no longer pursue them. If repentance and faith is like entering through a door, baptism is like firmly closing the door behind you.

### The faith reality of water baptism

This closing of the door can be a reality for us in faith. Colossians 2:12 says: *...having been buried with him in baptism and raised with him through your faith in the power of God, who raised him from the dead.* The text goes beyond simple obedience and links *faith* to the baptism verses.

This can give us a tool against the influence of the enemy. Not everyone has a definite date for conversion. Some do not know when their Christian life started, and for others it feels more of a gradual or ongoing process. Yet everyone can have a definite cut-off date: the date of baptism. If we put faith in the *fact* of baptism as well as in the *act* of baptism as a genuine spiritual cut-off—a Red Sea closure or a door firmly shut—we can be free from the enemy's power and influence.

**Footnote:** *When should I be baptised?* As soon as possible. Have a look at Acts 8:12; 36,37. Baptism is part of the *initiation* of the Christian life, and should not be delayed. It's a step towards maturity, not a reward for it.

## Review Questions on Chapter 2

1. All people need a Saviour.  TRUE or FALSE?
2. Give three reasons Jesus came from Luke 19:10; 1 John 3:5 & 8
3. According to Isaiah 53:6, what was placed from us on to Christ?
4. According to 2 Corinthians 5:21, what are we made in Christ?
5. What does the word "baptise" mean?
6. Unless you're baptised in water, you cannot be saved. TRUE or FALSE?
7. The will of God is that all believers are baptised in water. TRUE or FALSE?
8. Have you been baptised in water?
       If "NO", what should you do?

# THREE

# THE CHURCH AND RELATIONSHIPS

Sometimes when we speak of the Church in the New Testament, we use the term "The Early Church". Here is the earliest picture we have of the Church, from day 1:

> *They devoted themselves to the apostles' teaching and to the fellowship, to the breaking of bread and to prayer. Everyone was filled with awe, and many wonders and miraculous signs were done by the apostles. All the believers were together and had everything in common. Selling their possessions and goods, they gave to anyone as he had need. Every day they continued to meet together in the temple courts. They broke bread in their homes and ate together with glad and sincere hearts, praising God and enjoying the favour of all the people. And the Lord added to their number daily those who were being saved.* Acts 2:42-47

What *is* the Church? We know it's not a *building* (although many people use the word "church" when they mean "church building" in a very loose and unhelpful way). Many then think of the Church as a *meeting*, but that's not it either. When the meeting is over, the Church still exists. A better description might be: *a group of people who are related to Jesus and to each other*. The last phrase, "and to each other" is critically important. The Church is about relationships.

Eternal life is based on relationship. Jesus said: *"Now this is eternal life: that they may know you, the only true God, and Jesus Christ, whom you have sent."* (John 17:3) Relational reality is when the public meeting ends. If there were no meeting, would we still have a Church? We certainly *should* have—but only if we're building relationally. The network of relationships can act like a fishing net—helping us catch and keep new converts—and for the sake of evangelism in general. Jesus prayed, *"... that all of them may be one, Father, just as you are in me and I am in you. May they also be in us so that the world may believe that you have sent me."* (John 17:21)

In another place, He taught, *"By this all men will know that you are my disciples, if you love one another."* (John 13:35)

What's a relationship?    Try this: *A relationship is a bond of friendship between two persons.*    Relationships exist at different levels.  The basic level is that we might call *casual acquaintance*, and we can have very many relationships at that level.  The next level might be *friend.*  We would have fewer of these, but can still have many.  Some will have more than others.  This increased level gives more privileges in the relationship, and also more responsibilities.  We then move up the *close friend* level, and again the number of relationships we have at this level will vary.  Most people can sustain no more than about six close friendships at any given time.  Finally, we may have *intimate friends.*  Some may not have any of these, others may have one or two or three.  Few people can sustain more than three.  For married people, one would hope that the spouse was in this category.  And in that case, it would be generally unwise to have an intimate friend of the opposite gender apart from the spouse.

In the following three pictures of the Church we see the importance of relationships.


**The Church is the Family of God.**

Perhaps the relationship model that is easiest for us to identify with is the family.

> *For this reason I kneel before the Father, from whom his whole family in heaven and on earth derives its name.*
>
> *Ephesians 3:14,15*

> *How great is the love the Father has lavished on us, that we should be called children of God! And that is what we are!*                    1 John 3:1

> *For you did not receive a spirit that makes you a slave again to fear, but you received the Spirit of adoption. And by him we cry, "Abba, Father." The Spirit himself testifies with our spirit that we are God's children. Now if we are children, then we are heirs—heirs of God and co-heirs with Christ*                    Romans 8:15-17

We're not born into the family of God; we're *adopted*, and *placed* as sons or daughters.  Jesus is the only natural Son, and we are adopted by *grace* (God's unmerited favour).  If we're sons of God and God is our Father, then we're all brothers and sisters, and this is what the family means.  Jesus therefore is our older brother (see Hebrews 2:11).  We stand only by faith in Him.  *Yet to all who received him, to those who believed in his name, he gave the right to become children of God* (John 1:12).

Family is all about relationships.  A properly-functioning family will be united, committed, and pulling together in good times and in hard times.  All this is central to the vision of Liberty Church:

> *Our vision is for a family of believers, committed to God and to each other, where people of all ages are finding hope, coming to faith and growing in their relationship with God as we follow Christ together.*

## The Church is the Body of Christ.

The Scripture verses are particularly clear.

> *[11]It was he who gave some to be apostles, some to be prophets, some to be evangelists, and some to be pastors and teachers, [12]to prepare God's people for works of service, so that the body of Christ may be built up [13]until we all reach unity in the faith and in the knowledge of the Son of God and become mature, attaining to the whole measure of the fullness of Christ.*
> *[14]Then we will no longer be infants, tossed back and forth by the waves, and blown here and there by every wind of teaching and by the cunning and craftiness of men in their deceitful scheming. [15]Instead, speaking the truth in love, we will in all things grow up into him who is the Head, that is, Christ.  [16]From him the whole body, joined and held together by every supporting ligament, grows and builds itself up in love, as each part does its work.*                              Ephesians 4:11-16

> *And God placed all things under his feet and appointed him to be head over everything for the church, which is his body, the fullness of him who fills everything in every way.*                              Ephesians 1:22,23

> *Just as each of us has one body with many members, and these members do not all have the same function, so in*

*Christ we who are many form one body, and each member belongs to all the others.* Romans 12:4,5

*[12]The body is a unit, though it is made up of many parts; and though all its parts are many, they form one body. So it is with Christ. [13]For we were all baptised by one Spirit into one body—whether Jews or Greeks, slave or free—and we were all given the one Spirit to drink.*

*[14]Now the body is not made up of one part but of many. [15]If the foot should say, "Because I am not a hand, I do not belong to the body," it would not for that reason cease to be part of the body. [16]And if the ear should say, "Because I am not an eye, I do not belong to the body," it would not for that reason cease to be part of the body. [17]If the whole body were an eye, where would the sense of hearing be? If the whole body were an ear, where would the sense of smell be? [18]But in fact God has arranged the parts in the body, every one of them, just as he wanted them to be. [19]If they were all one part, where would the body be? [20]As it is, there are many parts, but one body.*

*[21]The eye cannot say to the hand, "I don't need you!" And the head cannot say to the feet, "I don't need you!" [22]On the contrary, those parts of the body that seem to be weaker are indispensable, [23]and the parts that we think are less honourable we treat with special honour. And the parts that are unpresentable are treated with special modesty, [24]while our presentable parts need no special treatment. But God has combined the members of the body and has given greater honour to the parts that lacked it, [25]so that there should be no division in the body, but that its parts should have equal concern for each other. [26]If one part suffers, every part suffers with it; if one part is honoured, every part rejoices with it.*

*[27]Now you are the body of Christ, and each one of you is a part of it.* 1 Corinthians 12:12-27

Each part is important, and has a purpose, value, gifting, and a unique contribution to make. We have equal worth and equal value, yet different function. It's a process of discovery—finding our place in the Body of Christ.  Maturity in the Body comes as each part does its work, and the whole is greater than the sum of the parts.

As for the parts of a body linked together, relationships are the *joints*, a joint being the meeting of two members.  It is in relationships that the body is connected, articulated and able to function.

## The Church is the Temple of the Holy Spirit.

Again, the biblical image is clear.

> *Consequently, you are no longer foreigners and aliens, but fellow citizens with God's people and members of God's household, built on the foundation of the apostles and prophets, with Christ Jesus himself as the chief cornerstone.  In him the whole building is joined together and rises to become a holy temple in the Lord.  And in him you too are being built together to become a dwelling in which God lives by his Spirit.*     Ephesians 2:19-22

> *Don't you know that you yourselves are God's temple and that God's Spirit lives in you?  If anyone destroys God's temple, God will destroy him; for God's temple is sacred, and you are that temple.*     1 Corinthians 3:16,17

> *As you come to him, the living Stone—rejected by men but chosen by God and precious to him—you also, like living stones, are being built into a spiritual house to be a holy priesthood, offering spiritual sacrifices acceptable to God through Jesus Christ.*     1 Peter 2:4,5

The Church is not a spiritual brick-pile.  A pile of bricks on a building site, like a group of Christians, has great potential.  But we need to build!  We are *living stones* and must be operated on by God—shaped, smoothed, and built together.

What holds these stones together?  Relationships.  We're cemented together by *love*, that is, the attitude of commitment.  If you ventured into a house built without cement, you would be nervous to say the least, fearful of a catastrophic collapse with you inside.  If we build a local Church like we would build a sandcastle, it too is likely to be here today and gone tomorrow.  Without relationships, we repel one another or fall apart.  With relationships, we attract one another or stick together.

What of the different levels of relationship?

As a brick in the wall, you have a relationship with every other brick, but you are closer to some than to others, specifically six. Perhaps these are close friends. Or perhaps you can picture them as two you support, two that support you, and two that keep you in check!

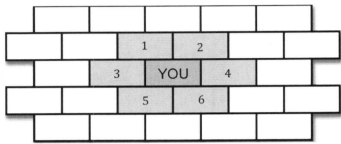

The Temple is where God dwells *by His Spirit*. Your primary relationship is with Jesus. Jesus is the cornerstone, on whom the whole thing rests. Yet Jesus is also the *whole*.

> *But the temple he had spoken of was his body.* John 2:21

In summary, the Church is all about relationships. We're the *Family of God*, the *Body of Christ*, the *Temple of the Holy Spirit*. We're related to Jesus, and to one another.

---

**Review Questions on Chapter 3**

1. A Church is a building. TRUE or FALSE?
2. A Church is a meeting. TRUE or FALSE?
3. What is a relationship?
4. What three pictures of the Church are outlined?
5. How do we enter the family of God?
6. If God is our Father, how do we relate to one another?
7. With whom is our primary relationship?
8. What are believers pictured as in 1 Peter 2:4,5?
9. We should seek to be in equally close relationship with everybody else in the Church. TRUE or FALSE?
10. It's quite acceptable to have very close friends and people we refuse to talk to in the same local Church. TRUE or FALSE?

## The "One Anothers" of the New Testament

This list of thirty "one anothers", if applied to life, gives the framework in which other-centredness is worked out.  Let's be doers of the Word towards one another.....

How we *are* towards one another

| | |
|---|---|
| 1. Be members of one another | Romans 12:5 |
| 2. Be devoted to one another | Romans 12:10a |
| 3. Honour one another above yourselves | Romans 12:10b |
| 4. Serve one another in love | Galatians 5:13 |
| 5. Be kind to one another | Ephesians 4:32 |
| 6. Submit to one another | Ephesians 5:21 |
| 7. Be clothed in humility towards one another | 1 Peter 5:5 |

How we *flow* with one another

| | |
|---|---|
| 8. Live in harmony with one another | Romans 12:16 |
| 9. Stop passing judgement on one another | Romans 14:13 |
| 10. Accept one another | Romans 15:7 |
| 11. Forgive one another | Ephesians 4:32 |
| 12. Bear with one another | Colossians 3:13 |
| 13. Don't grumble against one another | James 5:9 |

Things we do *with* one another

| | |
|---|---|
| 14. Rejoice with one another | Romans 12:15 |
| 15. Mourn with one another | Romans 12:15 |
| 16. Greet one another | Romans 16:16 |
| 17. Wait for one another | 1 Corinthians 11:33 |
| 18. Carry one another's burdens | Galatians 6:2 |
| 19. Don't slander one another | James 4:11 |
| 20. Fellowship with one another | 1 John 1:7 |

Things we do *to* one another

| | |
|---|---|
| 21. Admonish one another | Romans 15:14 |
| 22. Care for one another | 1 Corinthians 12:25 |
| 23. Build up one another | 1 Thessalonians 5:11 |
| 24. Encourage one another | Hebrews 3:13 |
| 25. Spur on one another | Hebrews 10:24 |
| 26. Confess faults to one another | James 5:16 |
| 27. Pray for one another | James 5:16 |
| 28. Offer hospitality to one another | 1 Peter 4:9 |
| 29. Minister by gifts to one another | 1 Peter 4:10 |

And above all...

| | |
|---|---|
| 30. Love one another | John 13:34,35 |

# FOUR

# POWER FROM ON HIGH

**KEY VERSE:** I am going to send you what my father has promised; but stay in the city until you have been clothed with power from on high.                                                    Luke 24:49

The last recorded words of Jesus on earth are found in Acts 1:8. He said:  *"...But you will receive power when the Holy Spirit comes on you; and you will be my witnesses in Jerusalem, and in all Judea and Samaria, and to the ends of the earth."*

Sometimes we talk about propositional truth.  Well, what we have here is *prepositional* truth!  Speaking of the Holy Spirit, Jesus predicted "another Counsellor to be with you forever" (John 14:16). Notice the preposition "with".  He then said that the Holy Spirit "lives with you and will be in you." (See John 14:17.)  We could say that at the time of speaking He lives *with* you, and at a time future to that He will be *in* you.  Clearly, we can see for example in Romans 8:11 that the Holy Spirit lives *in* us.  But then in Acts 1:8, Jesus speaks about the Holy Spirit coming *on* or *upon* us, a different preposition again.  Selwyn Hughes used to teach, "The Holy Spirit is *with* us to *convict*, *in* us to *convert*, and *upon* us to *clothe* [i.e. empower]."  It clearly seems to be the case that references to the Holy Spirit *upon* are consistently linked with the *power* of the Spirit.  We'll keep that in mind as we examine the Scriptures, looking at four relevant passages.

First of all, Pentecost:

> *¹When the day of Pentecost came, they were all together in one place. ²Suddenly a sound like the blowing of a violent wind came from heaven and filled the whole house where they were sitting. ³They saw what seemed to be tongues of fire that separated and came to rest on each of them. ⁴All of them were filled with the Holy Spirit and began to speak in other tongues as the Spirit enabled them.*

*5Now there were staying in Jerusalem God-fearing Jews from every nation under heaven. 6When they heard this sound, a crowd came together in bewilderment, because each one heard them speaking in his own language. 7Utterly amazed, they asked: "Are not all these men who are speaking Galileans? 8Then how is it that each of us hears them in his own native language? 9Parthians, Medes and Elamites; residents of Mesopotamia, Judea and Cappadocia, Pontus and Asia, 10Phrygia and Pamphylia, Egypt and the parts of Libya near Cyrene; visitors from Rome 11(both Jews and converts to Judaism); Cretans and Arabs — we hear them declaring the wonders of God in our own tongues!" 12Amazed and perplexed, they asked one another, "What does this mean?"*

*13Some, however, made fun of them and said, "They have had too much wine."*                    Acts 2:1-13

Notice that in verse 3, the tongues of fire came to rest *upon* them. In verse 4, the language is of being "filled with the Spirit", and yet Pentecost is clearly presented as the fulfilment of Acts 1:8, when the Holy Spirit would come *upon* them.   Clearly too they spoke in tongues.   On the basis of verses 8 to 11, it is sometimes contended that the disciples simply spoke, and that each hearer heard them in his own language.   This would make it a miracle of *hearing* rather than of *speaking*.   Although it sounds attractive at first, this does not fit.   It's clear from verse 4 that they *spoke* in other tongues before anyone heard them.   Besides, who was the Holy Spirit ON, the *speakers* or the *hearers*?

Secondly, Philip in Samaria:

*9Now for some time a man named Simon had practised sorcery in the city and amazed all the people of Samaria. He boasted that he was someone great, 10and all the people, both high and low, gave him their attention and exclaimed, "This man is the divine power known as the Great Power." 11They followed him because he had amazed them for a long time with his magic. 12But when they believed Philip as he preached the good news of the kingdom of God and the name of Jesus Christ, they were baptised, both men and women. 13Simon himself believed and was baptised. And he followed Philip everywhere, astonished by the great signs and miracles he saw.*

*14When the apostles in Jerusalem heard that Samaria had accepted the word of God, they sent Peter and John to them. 15When they arrived, they prayed for them that they might receive the Holy Spirit, 16because the Holy Spirit had not yet come upon any of them; they had simply been baptised into the name of the Lord Jesus. 17Then Peter and John placed their hands on them, and they received the Holy Spirit.*

*18When Simon saw that the Spirit was given at the laying on of the apostles' hands, he offered them money...*

Acts 8:9-18

This is an important passage, and there are three things to say. First, the Samaritans were clearly believers (see verse 12) and saved (Mark 16:16). Yet secondly it seems that in their response to the Gospel, there was something different—the *power* dimension was missing, perhaps for the first time. Peter and John added to the ministry by laying hands on the new converts, "because the Holy Spirit had not yet come upon any of them, and they received the Holy Spirit." The deficiency was made good. If this is indeed a correct understanding, notice the link again between the *power* dimension and the Holy Spirit coming *upon*. Thirdly, we are not told what tangibly happened or how they knew it, but we *are* told in verse 18 that it was *visible*—Simon *saw* it. His reaction was wrong, but his observation was correct. The importance of this passage is that it indicates a receiving of the Holy Spirit (and I suggest specifically the *power* of the Holy Spirit) subsequent to conversion.

Then we have Peter and Cornelius. Cornelius, a God-fearer, was supernaturally directed to send for Peter who would bring a message through which he and all his household would be saved (see Acts 11:14). In response Peter came and spoke:

*44While Peter was still speaking these words, the Holy Spirit came on all who heard the message. 45The circumcised believers who had come with Peter were astonished that the gift of the Holy Spirit had been poured out even on the Gentiles. 46For they heard them speaking in tongues and praising God. Then Peter said, 47"Can anyone keep these people from being baptised with*

> *water?   They have received the Holy Spirit just as we*
> *have."*                                             Acts 10:44-47

Notice, in verse 44, the Holy Spirit is again said to come *on* them. When Peter recounts this episode to the Church in Jerusalem he says: "As I began to speak, the Holy Spirit came *on* them as he had come *on* us at the beginning." (Acts 11:15, emphasis added.)   Linked with this is the observation that they spoke in tongues and praised God.

Fourthly, Paul at Ephesus.   But this story starts with Apollos at Ephesus:

> *[24]Meanwhile a Jew named Apollos, a native of Alexandria, came to Ephesus.   He was a learned man, with a thorough knowledge of the Scriptures.   [25]He had been instructed in the way of the Lord, and he spoke with great fervour and taught about Jesus accurately, though he knew only the baptism of John.   [26]He began to speak boldly in the synagogue.   When Priscilla and Aquila heard him, they invited him to their home and explained to him the way of God more adequately.*            Acts 18:24-26

For all the learning, something was deficient in the understanding of Apollos.  I suggest that it had to do with the dimension of the Holy Spirit and power.  His understanding was expanded by Priscilla and Aquila, as a result of which I would expect him to want to go to Corinth where all the action was.  Sure enough, he wants to go to Achaia, the province in which Corinth is located.

> *[27]When Apollos wanted to go to Achaia, the brothers encouraged him and wrote to the disciples there to welcome him.   On arriving, he was a great help to those who by grace had believed.   [28]For he vigorously refuted the Jews in public debate, proving from the Scriptures that Jesus was the Christ.*            Acts 18:27,28

So Apollos and the Corinthian Church seemed to be of mutual benefit to each other.  The story continues:

> *[19:1]While Apollos was at Corinth,* [so he indeed did go to Corinth] *Paul took the road through the interior and arrived at Ephesus.   There he found some disciples [2]and asked them, "Did you receive the Holy Spirit when you believed?"*

Some people have taken the view that these were not true Christian believers, but pre-Christians, disciples of John the Baptist, and that under Paul's ministry here they in fact are saved.  But this view does not stand up to scrutiny.  They are described in verse 1 as "disciples".  A study of the Book of Acts to this point will reveal that the word "disciples", without further comment, has been used consistently to mean "believers in and followers of Jesus".   Why would Luke, the author, suddenly change the use of the term without explanation in this chapter?   No, these are followers of Jesus (i.e. Christians), who are in some way deficient in a sense connected with the Holy Spirit, perhaps in a similar way to the believers in Acts 8 before Peter and John laid their hands on them.

> They answered, "No, we have not even heard that there is a Holy Spirit."
> *3So Paul asked, "Then what baptism did you receive?"*
> "John's baptism," they replied.

Does this sound familiar?  It's the same language as Acts 18:25.  These men must have been the result of the ministry of Apollos, who has naturally reproduced his own shortcomings in those he instructed, before Priscilla and Aquila explained to him the way of God more adequately.  Paul sets the men straight.

> *4Paul said, "John's baptism was a baptism of repentance.  He told the people to believe in the one coming after him, that is, in Jesus."  5On hearing this, they were baptised into the name of the Lord Jesus.  6When Paul placed his hands on them, the Holy Spirit came on them, and they spoke in tongues and prophesied.  7There were about twelve men in all.*

Note in verse 6, we're told that the Holy Spirit came **on** them, in language linked with power as elsewhere.  As a result, they spoke in tongues and prophesied.

These four passages, then, paint a consistent picture.  At this stage, we can make four observations:

- Receiving the power of the Spirit is linked to the Holy Spirit coming ON.
- Receiving the power of the Spirit can be at conversion or later.
- Receiving the power of the Spirit is somehow visible.

- Receiving the power of the Spirit is closely linked with speaking in tongues.

This receiving "power from on high" was clearly a feature of the early Church.  However as the years became centuries, much of this awareness and experience seems to have been lost, although throughout Church history there have always been groups and individuals who have experienced the power and the gifts of the Holy Spirit.  A renewed emphasis came at the beginning of the twentieth century with the Pentecostal revival and the beginning of the Pentecostal Church.  It continued throughout the century with the Latter Rain movement, and then the Charismatic movement beginning around 1960, and growing around the world.  Liberty Church in Dunfermline was begun in 1979 out of this movement as a charismatic church.  The Church's first slogan was "a Charismatic Ministry in Your Community."

My own story is that I learned of the Charismatic movement from books, notably "The Spirit Bade Me Go" by David Du Plessis, and "Nine O'Clock in the Morning" by Dennis Bennett.  My investigations became all the more urgent when I discovered to my surprise that I was married to someone who spoke in tongues!  I began to seek this empowering experience, but nothing seemed to happen.  I found myself looking at other people, people I knew had this experience, and it was as if I could see them wearing a diver's helmet with an oxygen line snaking upwards, like a hotline to heaven.  I knew they had something that I didn't have, and I was jealous!  After a couple of unsuccessful attempts to meet with someone I thought could help, I knelt down one night by myself at the kitchen table, and asked God to empower me with the Holy Spirit.  In line with all the testimonies I had heard, I expected to begin to speak in tongues.  So I opened my mouth — but nothing came out.  I suppose I expected the Holy Spirit to come upon me, take my voice, and make it say something.  At the time, I did not understand that we speak, but the Holy Spirit gives the utterance (see Acts 2:4).

Still nothing seemed to happen that night at the kitchen table.  Yet for the next three days, I seemed to feel unusually happy; and a simple old worship song that I didn't even like kept going round and round in my head: "The joy of the Lord is my strength."  It was some weeks after this before I spoke in tongues for the first time.  However, looking back, I believe I was empowered by the Holy Spirit (that is, that the Holy Spirit came upon me) that night kneeling at the kitchen table.

Does the promise include speaking in tongues?  Some people would not be convinced that they had indeed been empowered by the Spirit unless they had spoken in tongues.  On the other hand, some people have declined to ask to be empowered by the Spirit, or been hesitant to do so, because they are unwilling to speak in tongues.  Both are asking the wrong question.  The question is not, "*Must* I speak in tongues?" but rather, "*May* I speak in tongues?"  Over the years, speaking in tongues has been a very divisive and much misunderstood gift.  Yet it seems very central to the New Testament experience.

Reviewing the Scripture passages, in Acts 2 at Pentecost they clearly spoke in tongues.  In Acts 10, they spoke in tongues and praised God, and in Acts 19 they spoke in tongues and prophesied.  In Acts 8, there is no direct mention of tongues, but it is clear that some evidence of empowering was perceptible, which Simon saw.  It is possible that this was, or included, tongues.  One could say, whenever the evidence is specified, tongues is included.  In addition, we know that Paul spoke in tongues.  He told the Corinthians, "I thank God that I speak in tongues more than all of you." (1 Corinthians 14:18)

Why is it good to speak in tongues?  First, it's good because it's *normal*, in the sense that the New Testament knows of no other kind of believer.  Secondly, it edifies or builds up the believer (1 Corinthians 14:4).  Thirdly, it blesses or praises God (1 Corinthians 14:16).  Fourthly, it releases prayer (1 Corinthians 14:14,15, and also Romans 8:23,26).

In summary, receiving the power of the Holy Spirit is linked to the Holy Spirit coming ON; it can be at conversion, or later; it comes with evidence or is somehow visible; and it is closely linked with speaking in tongues.  Additionally from Acts 8 and Acts 19, we see that the empowering may be appropriated through prayer and the laying on of hands.  If we ask, "*Must* I speak in tongues?" the answer is no.  But it's better to ask the question, "*May* I speak in tongues?"  And the answer to *that* question is apparently yes.

Lastly, don't forget the final key to being clothed with power from on high:

> *"So I say to you: Ask and it will be given to you; seek and you will find; knock and the door will be opened to you.*

*For everyone who asks receives; he who seeks finds; and to him who knocks, the door will be opened.*

*"Which of you fathers, if your son asks for a fish, will give him a snake instead?  Or if he asks for an egg, will give him a scorpion?  If you then, though you are evil, know how to give good gifts to your children, how much more will your Father in heaven give the Holy Spirit to those who ask him!"*                                    Luke 11:9-13

The final key is: ask.

---

### Gifts of the Holy Spirit

As well as the power of the Spirit, we believe that the gifts of the Spirit are available to believers today.  These are found in 1 Corinthians 12:7-11.  Verse 7 indicates that these are aspects of the invisible Holy Spirit making Himself in some sense visible or observable; and they are given not to endorse or reward an individual, but for the common good.

There are nine listed:

1. Word of wisdom
2. Word of knowledge
3. Faith
4. Gifts of healing
5. Working of miracles
6. Prophecy
7. Distinguishing of spirits
8. Speaking in tongues
9. Interpretation of tongues

We are encouraged to desire these gifts earnestly, and to seek to excel in gifts that build up the church (see 1 Corinthians 14:1,12).  Yet He gives them to each one, just as He determines (1 Corinthians 12:11).

# FIVE

# THE KINGDOM OF GOD AND HEALING

### "TWO KINGDOMS" DIAGRAM

### SALVATION

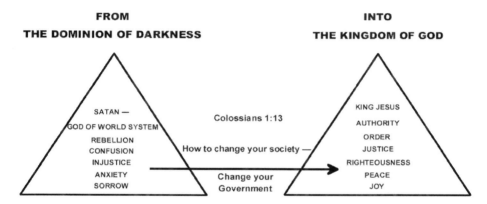

#### The Kingdom of God

This helpful diagram pictures *salvation* as coming *out* of the dominion of darkness, and *into* the Kingdom of God. The first question to ask is: What is the Kingdom of God?

The Kingdom of God is God's rule and reign. The original words in the Bible text indicate that it does not principally refer to the *realm*, that is the territory over which the King rules; or the *subjects*, that is the people over whom the King rules. It refers first of all the actual rule, the government, the kingship of the King.

What happens to people becoming Christians? According to the text mentioned:

> *For He rescued us from the domain of darkness, and transferred us to the kingdom of His beloved Son*
>
> Colossians 1:13 NAS

We've been transferred or translated from the left triangle to the right. Notice the characteristics of where we were: Satan, the "god" of the world system, is pulling the strings.  The characteristics are rebellion, confusion, injustice, anxiety and sorrow.  In the other triangle, King Jesus rules, and His rule is characterised by authority (rather than rebellion), order (rather than confusion), justice (as opposed to injustice), and righteousness, peace and joy in the Holy Spirit (see Romans 14:17).  To change your society, you must change your government.  Entering the Kingdom of God is coming under the Lordship of Jesus Christ.

And what in this sense is the meaning of the Lordship of Jesus Christ?  It's Jesus ruling supreme over every area of your life.  The fact is that something will rule us, perhaps habits or desires.  Unless we settle the issue of Lordship, it's hard to make much progress in the Christian life.

Perhaps surprisingly, the place of true liberty is under Lordship.  At first this sounds odd.  Lordship sounds like a place of restriction where options are limited, and we're not free at all.  But what is true freedom?  How do we understand it?  We could put it this way.  The strategy of the enemy is to get you into bondage, any bondage will do.  To express it in terms of a football match, he wants you out of the game.  If he can get you injured or disqualified, that'll do it.  If he can provoke you into committing offences so that you get a red card, that will do instead.  If he can tempt you to pick up the ball and stomp off home in a huff, he'll settle for that.  Any bondage will do that gets you out of the game.  The strategy of the enemy is to get you into bondage.  On the other hand, the strategy of the Holy Spirit is set you free from all controlling influences, to free you to God. *"...where the Spirit of the Lord is, there is freedom"* (2 Corinthians 3:17).

Ponder this for a moment: *True freedom is not the right to do what you like, but the power to do what you ought.*  Under Lordship, you're truly free to do what you *ought* to do.

## Healing and Kingdom Order

How does the Kingdom of God relate to healing?  This is an important question, because health and healing are important to everybody.  Notice again that *order* is a characteristic of God's Kingdom, and correspondingly *disorder* is a characteristic of the dominion of darkness.  Those who live in a tall building hope the lift is in good working order, and the last thing they welcome is a sign on it that says, "Out of Order".  Similarly, health corresponds to "order";

sickness is "out of order". The dominion of darkness is characterised by disorder. *Disorder* implies *out of order*, which in turn implies that health is normal.

We know this intuitively. If we cut one of our fingers, we have an expectation of healing, not of permanent disablement! If we scratch our car, we don't expect the scratch to "heal" all by itself, but if we cut our finger, we do. And if the wound in the finger does *not* heal, we would think that was abnormal; because health and healing are normal.

God's way is healing. If we break an arm or a leg, what do doctors do? They position the limb correctly, immobilise it, and wait for the bone to heal. It heals itself, because God's way is healing.

Where does sickness come from? The Bible seems to indicate that sickness entered the world at the Fall. Satan infected mankind with his rebellion, mankind fell into sin, and all creation began to decay.

> *Through these he has given us his very great and precious promises, so that through them you may participate in the divine nature and escape the corruption in the world caused by evil desires.*          2 Peter 1:4

> *The creation waits in eager expectation for the sons of God to be revealed. For the creation was subjected to frustration, not by its own choice, but by the will of the one who subjected it, in hope that the creation itself will be liberated from its bondage to decay and brought into the glorious freedom of the children of God.*
>                                                        Romans 8:19-21

To say that sin is the source of sickness is not to say that if I'm sick it must be my own fault. I'm not necessarily sick because of *my* sin, but because of sin in general. The condition of the world is fallen—we live life on a fallen planet. The rain falls on the righteous and the unrighteous. Viruses, and so on, are in the world and can be caught.

Additionally, sickness can be caused directly or indirectly by evil spirits. In Acts 10:38 we have, "*... God anointed Jesus of Nazareth with the Holy Spirit and power, and how he went around doing good and healing all who were under the power of the devil, because God was with him.*" Note that those "under the power of the devil" were released by *healing*.

> *[10]On a Sabbath Jesus was teaching in one of the synagogues, [11]and a woman was there who had been crippled by a spirit for eighteen years. She was bent over and could not straighten up at all. [12]When Jesus saw her, he called her forward and said to her, "Woman, you are set free from your infirmity." [13]Then he put his hands on her, and immediately she straightened up and praised God.*
>
> *[14]Indignant because Jesus had healed on the Sabbath, the synagogue ruler said to the people, "There are six days for work. So come and be healed on those days, not on the Sabbath."*
>
> *[15]The Lord answered him, "You hypocrites! Doesn't each of you on the Sabbath untie his ox or donkey from the stall and lead it out to give it water? [16]Then should not this woman, a daughter of Abraham, whom Satan has kept bound for eighteen long years, be set free on the Sabbath day from what bound her?"*        Luke 13:10-16

In this passage, the language is the language of healing. Yet the problem is clearly caused by an evil spirit (see verse 11).

Sickness is not sourced in the Kingdom of God. It may sometimes affect those who are in the Kingdom of God, but it's not sourced there. God is the source of *health*.

## God's will to heal

After the Exodus, God revealed something of Himself in the words, "...I am the LORD who heals you." (Exodus 15:26)  Later, in the opening of Psalm 103, we find:

> *Praise the LORD, O my soul; all my inmost being, praise his holy name. Praise the LORD, O my soul, and forget not all his benefits—who forgives all your sins and heals all your diseases*

Then in the well-known words of Isaiah 53:3-5

> *He was despised and rejected by men, a man of sorrows, and familiar with suffering. Like one from whom men hide their faces he was despised, and we esteemed him not. Surely he took up our infirmities and carried our sorrows, yet we considered him stricken by God, smitten*

*by him, and afflicted.    But he was pierced for our transgressions, he was crushed for our iniquities; the punishment that brought us peace was upon him, and by his wounds we are healed.*

These words are picked up again in Matthew's gospel:

*When evening came, many who were demon-possessed were brought to him, and he drove out the spirits with a word and healed all the sick.    This was to fulfil what was spoken through the prophet Isaiah: "He took up our infirmities and carried our diseases."*    Matthew 8:16,17

In overview we could say that from the foundation of the world, God is *Jehovah Rapha*, the Lord who heals.    It was ratified in the public ministry and Cross of Jesus Christ, and is now available by faith to New Covenant believers.    Healing is the will of God.

We have to believe this.    Otherwise, we'd better stop taking medicine or we might get healed against the will of God!    This sounds ridiculous, and indeed it is.    But it remains that unless we're confident it's God's will that we're healed, taking medicine may be us attempting to go against the will of God.

In this sense of the will of God, we have to consider Matthew 6:10, the heart of the Lord's Prayer, "Your kingdom come, your will be done on earth as it is in heaven."    Clearly God's will does not always happen automatically.    We have to pray for it; and any answered prayer makes the point.    According to the will of God, we may have to pray or ask or speak or obey in His will, and that appropriates and releases what's *willed* in heaven to be *done* on earth.

## Jesus' healing ministry

There are forty-one recorded healings of Jesus in the Gospels. Let's take a glance through Matthew's gospel:

*Jesus went throughout Galilee, teaching in their synagogues, preaching the good news of the kingdom, and healing every disease and sickness among the people.  News about him spread all over Syria, and people brought to him all who were ill with various diseases, those suffering severe pain, the demon-possessed, those having seizures, and the paralysed, and he healed them.*
Matthew 4:23,24

*When evening came, many who were demon-possessed were brought to him, and he drove out the spirits with a word and healed all the sick.*                    Matthew 8:16

*Jesus went through all the towns and villages, teaching in their synagogues, preaching the good news of the kingdom and healing every disease and sickness.*
                                                          Matthew 9:35

*Heal the sick, raise the dead, cleanse those who have leprosy, drive out demons. Freely you have received, freely give.*                                Matthew 10:8

*Aware of this, Jesus withdrew from that place.  Many followed him, and he healed all their sick.*  Matthew 12:15

*When Jesus landed and saw a large crowd, he had compassion on them and healed their sick.*
                                                          Matthew 14:14

*... and begged him to let the sick just touch the edge of his cloak, and all who touched him were healed.*
                                                          Matthew 14:36

*Great crowds came to him, bringing the lame, the blind, the crippled, the mute and many others, and laid them at his feet; and he healed them.*        Matthew 15:30

*The blind and the lame came to him at the temple, and he healed them.*                            Matthew 21:14

It seems that all who came to Him were healed.

## What to do if you get sick

Pray first.  Seek Jesus to heal you through the power of the Holy Spirit.  Having done that, be open to the possibility that God may heal you through doctors if He so chooses.  Once we've established that our faith is in the Source, help can come through many avenues.

Note too our responsibilities in James 5:14-16:

*Is any one of you sick?  He should call the elders of the church to pray over him and anoint him with oil in the name of the Lord.  And the prayer offered in faith will make the sick person well; the Lord will raise him up.  If he has sinned, he will be forgiven.  Therefore confess your sins to each other and pray for each other so that you may be healed.  The prayer of a righteous man is powerful and effective.*

It's always right to pray for healing if you're sick.

# LORDSHIP

**KEY VERSE:** That if you confess with your mouth, "Jesus is Lord," and believe in your heart that God raised Him from the dead, you will be saved.  For it is with your heart that you believe and are justified, and it is with your mouth that you confess and are saved.                                                Romans 10:9,10

## Jesus is Lord

What does this statement mean?  It's really a way of saying several things at once.  First, it's a way of declaring that Jesus is God, who is known as The Lord in the Old Testament.  Secondly, it can be a declaration that Jesus is the Anointed One, the Messiah, the One whose coming they had long predicted.  But most of the time we understand it to be a declaration that Jesus is our Master, our Ruler, our King, our Boss, the One we submit to and obey.

People sometimes acknowledge Jesus as a good example, or as a great teacher, or even as Saviour.  These things are true, but also He is *Lord*.

## Why you should acknowledge Jesus as Lord

Because that's who He is!  Romans 14:9 tells us that the reason Jesus died and returned to life was that He might be Lord, Lord of both the dead and the living.  He humbled Himself, and became obedient to death on the cross; therefore God exalted Him to the highest place and gave Him the name above every name: Lord!

## Lordship must be total

Jesus must be Lord of all, or He's not Lord at all.  If we try to make Him 50% Lord, or 90% Lord, or even 99% Lord, we are still retaining control over which areas are "off limits" to Him — and so He's not Lord.  The challenge is to follow with an undivided heart (see Psalm 86:11,12).

This is not unattainable.  It does not imply instant perfection, but a decision in principle to follow, submit and change in an ongoing way as revelation comes.

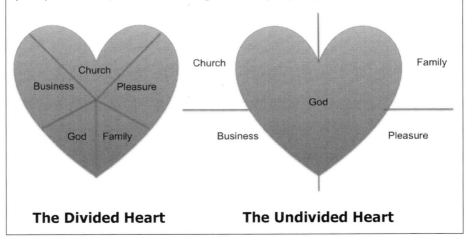

**The Divided Heart**          **The Undivided Heart**

# SIX

# WALKING IN FORGIVENESS

They're Christians and they sound impressively mature in conversation. They seem to know a lot, and "have it all together". Yet in situations of pressure or conflict or tension, they may unexpectedly act in very childish ways. It most often seems to happen in situations of relational difficulty, when things go wrong, and the true maturity level is revealed.

How do we handle relational difficulties? What happens when things go wrong? It's very easy to get miffed, or offended, or to feel wronged, and become caustic and bitter. How do we avoid this? We can't avoid the problems, but what we *can* do is respond correctly when the problems come. And the key response that we need to make is, in a single word, forgiveness.

Jesus taught His followers, "If your brother sins, rebuke him, and if he repents, forgive him. If he sins against you seven times in a day, and seven times comes back to you and says, 'I repent,' forgive him." It was a hard lesson. No wonder they responded by saying, "Increase our faith!" (See Luke 17:3-5.) The Amplified Bible expands the phrase "forgive him" as "give up resentment and consider the offence as recalled and annulled."

How can we do that? How can we do it to the same person seven times in a day?

There are two sides to the problem. On the one hand, Jesus said:

*And when you stand praying, if you hold anything against anyone, forgive him, so that your Father in heaven may forgive you your sins.* Mark 11:25

When you stand praying, if *you* hold anything against *anyone*, that is, *he* has wronged *you*, or you *think* he has, then forgive him *as you stand praying*.

On the other hand, Jesus also said:

*Therefore, if you are offering your gift at the altar and there remember that your brother has something against you, leave your gift there in front of the altar. First go and*

*be reconciled to your brother; then come and offer your*
*gift.*                                                    Matthew 5:23,24

Here you remember that your brother has something against *you*,
that is, *you* have wronged *him*, then leave your gift at the altar and
go sort it out.

In the first case, the other party may never know.  In the second
case, he must.  We cannot be right with God unless we are right with
people.

## The parable of the unmerciful servant

The major teaching here comes from the parable of the unmerciful
servant.  Here it is in full:

> $^{21}$*Then Peter came to Jesus and asked, "Lord, how*
> *many times shall I forgive my brother when he sins*
> *against me?  Up to seven times?"*
> $^{22}$*Jesus answered, "I tell you, not seven times, but*
> *seventy-seven times.*
> $^{23}$*"Therefore, the kingdom of heaven is like a king who*
> *wanted to settle accounts with his servants.   $^{24}$As he*
> *began the settlement, a man who owed him ten thousand*
> *talents was brought to him.   $^{25}$Since he was not able to*
> *pay, the master ordered that he and his wife and his*
> *children and all that he had be sold to repay the debt.*
> $^{26}$*"The servant fell on his knees before him.  'Be patient*
> *with me,' he begged, 'and I will pay back everything.'*
> $^{27}$*The servant's master took pity on him, cancelled the*
> *debt and let him go.*
> $^{28}$*"But when that servant went out, he found one of his*
> *fellow servants who owed him a hundred denarii.  He*
> *grabbed him and began to choke him.  'Pay back what*
> *you owe me!' he demanded.*
> $^{29}$*"His fellow servant fell to his knees and begged him,*
> *'Be patient with me, and I will pay you back.'*
> $^{30}$*"But he refused.  Instead, he went off and had the*
> *man thrown into prison until he could pay the debt.*
> $^{31}$*When the other servants saw what had happened, they*
> *were greatly distressed and went and told their master*
> *everything that had happened.*

*32"Then the master called the servant in. 'You wicked servant,' he said, 'I cancelled all that debt of yours because you begged me to. 33Shouldn't you have had mercy on your fellow servant just as I had on you?' 34In anger his master turned him over to the jailers to be tortured, until he should pay back all he owed.*

*35"This is how my heavenly Father will treat each of you unless you forgive your brother from your heart."*

Matthew 18:21-35

As the story opens, Peter is looking for a standard—*"Up to seven times?"*  The rabbis said three, so seven was generous!  Jesus' response was shocking—*"I tell you, not seven times, but seventy-seven times."*  Or perhaps the translation should be "seventy times seven".  This is not to say that Peter should keep a tally all the way up to 490 times, and then refuse to forgive on the 491st!  It indicates "times beyond counting", a limitless, infinite spirit of forgiveness.  To illustrate and clarify, He tells the parable.

The first servant owed ten thousand talents, which is the equivalent of 200,000 years' wages, a huge sum, indicating the idea of an unpayable debt.  The servant begged for mercy, promising with good intentions to repay the debt.  In response, the master cancelled the debt, and let him go.  In spite of this, the servant found a fellow servant who owed him a hundred denarii.  This was the equivalent of four months' wages.  It was certainly not insignificant, but it was payable, and negligible by comparison to the huge debt he had just been released from.  The fellow servant begged for mercy using the same words, and yet the first servant responded harshly, showing no mercy.  This behaviour distressed the other servants, who told the master.  The master's response was to call the unmerciful servant to account on the basis that he should have shown mercy as mercy had been shown to him.  In anger the master turned him over to the tormentors until he should pay back all he owed.  It's important to see that what he owed now was not ten thousand talents—that debt had been cancelled.  What he owed was to show mercy as mercy had been shown to him.

The parable is about forgiveness, not monetary debt, even though it uses that language, as Jesus makes clear in verse 35.  But think for a moment: at the end of the parable, where is the "fellow servant"?  He is still in the debtors' prison, where the first servant put him, as was his right.  The master did not release him.  That was for the first servant to do; and in the process he would release himself.

We owed an unpayable debt, but in the mercy of the Master it has been cancelled.  We have been forgiven!  If anyone now wrongs us, it's in the hundred denarii category at best.  Looked at in isolation, it may not be insignificant, but in comparison it's negligible.  Having been forgiven the much greater debt, to hold unforgiveness against others is ludicrous, unfair and ungrateful.

*Be kind and compassionate to one another, forgiving each other, just as in Christ God forgave you.* (Ephesians 4:32)  We forgive at the level we've been forgiven.  Once we know how much we ourselves have been forgiven, we have no excuse.

Our unforgiveness of others has consequences, both for them and for us.  We imprison others—keep in mind that the fellow servant is not released—we lock them up in that area.  Also we ourselves suffer.  We're liable to be consigned to the tormentors until we forgive, which is the debt now.

We cannot be definitive about what the tormentors are; but anyone in the healing ministry pretty quickly develops a motivation to avoid unforgiveness, because they have seen what unforgiveness can do.  On the basis of observation, unforgiveness can manifest itself as unanswered prayer, or a feeling of no victory, or a sense of being able to observe others interacting yet being unable to participate, or not hearing from God, or a sickness that won't seem to go away, or developed conditions like arthritis (that is *not* to say that all arthritis is caused by unforgiveness, but some is), or worse things in more extreme cases.

## What forgiveness is and is not

First, forgiveness is not an *occasion*, but a *lifestyle*.  We cannot take several days or several weeks to work up to forgiving someone.  The need is too great for that!  The more relationally clear we are, the more it can feel like we're constantly forgiving; until it becomes a lifestyle and that's that.

Secondly, it's not a response to an apology.  To apologise means to express regret for a fault.  It's a description of one's *feelings*.  Feeling sorry or saying sorry is not the issue.  One can be sorry for a great variety of reasons.  Some apologies essentially say, "I'm sorry for my faults.  It's just the way I am."  That attitude still dodges taking responsibility.

Thirdly, forgiveness is not what we perceive as the wise thing to do, but rather it's *obedience*. Some may reason, "I see the benefits of forgiving. This might help. I think I'll take a risk and forgive." This may get us to the right place, and therefore work in a limited sense. But it's based in a wrong motivation. True forgiveness is not experimental, but a response of obedience. Why do I forgive? Here's the phrase: The Master commanded me to forgive. We may say in response, "I don't want to," but that does not matter.

In counselling people one-to-one, I frequently hear a reaction that says, "I can't forgive that person." When I hear that, I generally look the person in the eyes and say, "I hear you saying, 'I can't forgive.' Let me tell you what I think you mean. You mean, 'I *won't* forgive.'" Sometimes the person will look as if about to erupt at this and ready to throw something at me. But the moment passes, and then I hear, "You're right." The issue is not the *ability* to forgive. It's a matter of the *will*.

Fourthly, forgiveness is not issued on the basis of *fruit*. Fred says to Joe, "I was wrong. Please forgive me." Joe replies, "I've heard it all before. Show me some evidence of change, and then I might forgive you." It's easy to be sceptical, particularly if the person concerned has asked for forgiveness several times before for the same thing; and it's understandable. Yet we cannot require and wait for the fruit of repentance to show that it's real. We can't do that seven times in one day! (See Luke 17:4, referred to above.)

Fifthly, forgiveness is not about feelings. It has nothing to do with feelings. Sometimes we feel better and mistake that for forgiveness. Sometimes we don't feel anything, and therefore don't forgive. We may say, "I can't be a hypocrite. I can't fake it." But forgiveness is not a feeling. It's a deliberate decision, a conscious choice, an act of the will.

What *is* forgiveness? There are two further things to say. First, it's rooted in and is a response to God's forgiveness of *us*. If we're struggling with it, it may therefore be helpful to meditate on how much we ourselves have been forgiven by God.

Secondly, forgiveness is a decision of the will, which says: "I release you, and I will not hold this against you in the future." It means we keep no files of forgiven offences. It means that every time we meet a forgiven person it's a fresh encounter with no baggage of offences from the past. It's a challenge to walk in forgiveness!

There's a common phrase "forgive and forget". In response, some say, "I still remember, so I must not have forgiven." But let's consider for a moment: can God forget? The answer is no. Things cannot "slip God's mind". He cannot misplace or erase facts. Yet God can and does forgive! He cannot forget what He's forgiven, but He chooses to remember it no more. That's a better phrase, and it works for us too. Once we've forgiven someone for some real or perceived offence, we choose to remember it no more. That's the challenge of walking in forgiveness.

## Whom we may need to forgive

It is generally unwise to play "hunt the problem", in this case to dig about in our memories of the past looking for areas where unforgiveness may lurk. However, it may be helpful to take time to pray something like, "Lord, I ask You to show me any people I need to forgive." Then pause in prayer, and see if any faces or situations come to mind. If so, simply deal with them as appropriate, and walk on. In some cases, this may be a process that lasts for some time, as the Lord reveals situations at a rate we can handle. At the end of it there will be much greater relational clarity. But it's not over, because we're walking in forgiveness, and the walk continues.

# SEVEN

# RESOLVING CONFLICTS

# AND REPAIRING BREACHES

If there is a problem, whatever it is, the best general advice is to deal with it. If not dealt with, the problem simply gets worse. If a car is beginning to rust, it's best dealt with quickly before the rust spreads. In the case of medical conditions such as cancer, contain the problem in as small an area as possible, and then deal with it. Often the most dangerous wound is one that bleeds inwardly, under the surface, unseen. What's true of the human body is also true of the Church, the Body of Christ. Relationship issues such as irritations, misunderstandings, accusations, conflicts and breaches must be identified, then contained and dealt with, before the damage spreads and infects the whole Body. It's easy for arguments, disputes and factions to form around half-truths, mistaken impressions, unfounded assumptions and just plain gossip, resulting in conflicts and breaches, with the relational fabric of the Church being torn apart. Nobody wants that, and neither is it necessary. Yet care and diligence are required to prevent it. There are principles to learn and apply.

It's better to be a peacekeeper than a troublemaker! Yet keeping the peace can sometimes lead us to ignore our responses and suppress our reactions, fuelling a bigger blow-up in the future. Rather than a peace*keeper*, it's better to be a peace*maker*. One of the characteristics of a peacemaker is refusing to be offended.

We need safety factors to stop things going wrong. This chapter is a safety-factor teaching in four stages. The further along in the stages we are, the less likely we are to *be* there. Yet all the stages are important to know and consider.

> *[15]"If your brother sins against you, go and show him his fault, just between the two of you. If he listens to you, you have won your brother over. [16]But if he will not listen, take one or two others along, so that 'every matter*

*may be established by the testimony of two or three witnesses.' [17]If he refuses to listen to them, tell it to the church; and if he refuses to listen even to the church, treat him as you would a pagan or a tax collector.*

Matthew 18:15-17

## Stage 1: The approach individually

"If your brother sins against you, go and show him his fault just between the two of you." Go in the right attitude, not to complain but to *gain*. The idea must not be to win the argument, but to win the *brother*, or of course, the *sister*, as the case may be.

It's important that we *go*, face to face, in private, you and him alone. In other words, don't write letters or e-mails or some form of text message. There's a great tendency to try to deal with it in writing, sometimes for practical reasons, but also because we think we can communicate better in writing, and if we talk face to face "it might come out wrong". However, the reverse is true. If misunderstood face to face, we have the immediate opportunity to clarify. The written confrontation is more problematic. You may know exactly what you meant by what you wrote. But you have no control over how the other person understands it. He may "hear" something very different from what you "said", and yet you don't know that. The result may be to make the problem very much worse! Misinterpretation is a grave danger.

Another reason not to attempt the approach in writing is that some things simply shouldn't be in print. A third reason is that writing makes it too easy for us, because it avoids the need for the moral courage to say it face to face. Finally, there is always a danger of the written message falling into the wrong hands. A letter may be left lying around where it can be read by others, an e-mail address may be shared or not confidential, and a text may easily be sent to the wrong person.

Our natural tendency if we think someone has wronged us is to tell someone else altogether, either simply to complain, or in the hope that that person will do something about it because we haven't got the bottle. This is *wrong!* The unfolding principle is: involve as few people as possible.

Suppose you lend your next-door neighbour your lawnmower. As times passes, you're surprised to note that he doesn't return it. If as a result you tell your neighbour on the other side, "He stole my lawnmower!", this is wrong.  You don't *know* that.  He may simply have forgotten.

Someone may come to you with an unsettling report and say, "John said you did such-and-such."  But John may not have said that at all.  If you believe it without checking, and act on it, perhaps by blabbing to someone else again, you have just compounded the problem several times.  What should you do?  Take it back to source.  Go to John and ask if he did say that.  He may well say no.  Or he may even say something like, "No, I didn't say that.  But I did say *this*, and I can see how he may have picked it up wrongly."  In the lawnmower case, speak to your neighbour who borrowed your lawnmower before you speak to anyone else about the matter.  Take it back to source.  Then you know what you're dealing with—if anything!

It's the Act 1 Finale of Gilbert and Sullivan's comic opera "Iolanthe".  On stage conversing are 24-year-old Strephon and Iolanthe, his mother.  The mother however is a fairy, and appears as if she's seventeen.  It's a situation that looks like something else.  Creeping on at the back of the stage are Strephon's fiancée Phyllis, and two noble lords.  They have understandably misread the situation!  Strephon sings tenderly to his apparently 17-year-old mother, "When darkly looms the day, and all is dull and grey, to chase the gloom away on thee I'll call."  At the back, Phyllis asks a noble lord who is straining to overhear, "What was that?"  He replies, "I think I heard him say that on a rainy day, to while the time away on her he'd call."  The gentlemen of the chorus then repeat his misheard statement.  Meanwhile, with equal tenderness, Iolanthe replies to her son, "When tempests wreck thy bark, and all is drear and dark, if thou shouldst need an ark, I'll give thee one."  Phyllis asks the other noble lord, "What was that?"  He replies, "I heard the minx remark she'd meet him after dark inside St James's Park and give him one!"  The gentlemen of the chorus then repeat this apparently scandalous revelation.  It's a funny scene.

But they'd got it wrong.  They'd misheard, misread and misunderstood, and then passed on the misinformation.  And that's often what happens in churches.  People overhear, mishear or misinterpret, inject their own assumptions or fears, and tell other people, who assume what they are told is true, and then they tell others.  Before long everyone seems to be upset and arguing!  Many times, I have had to "unpack the chains"—asking, "What did you hear?  Who did you hear it from?"—then going back to that person and asking the same thing—and so on.  It can be like "Chinese whispers", where things change in the telling.  And it can be interesting detective work to find where it all came from, who it was who misheard a comment, or misconstrued a situation, and set things in motion.  The next problem is that all the people who have been affected have to be set right, in order that peace and health may return to the Body.  The effect of all this spread of misinformation is extremely destructive of relationships; and it never would have happened if those concerned had responded according to the biblical principles.  These things really matter.  If we receive an untrue report, we're receiving a slanderous accusation; and if we then tell it to someone else, we're gossip-mongering and discord-sowing.  The effect is serious and the sin grievous.

"Go and show him his fault just between the two of you."  Expect success.  Most problems between two people are known only to one.  If successful, the matter is put right, forgiveness is extended and received where necessary, and that's an end of it.  It should not be mentioned again.

## Stage 2: The approach with witnesses

If Stage 1 is unsuccessful, don't despair or hate the person.  Try again.

Matthew 18:16 says:

> But if he will not listen, take one or two others along, so that "every matter may be established by the testimony of two or three witnesses."

Deuteronomy 19:15 is the verse being referred to here.  It tells us that we need two or three, so we take one or two others along.  The same principle is in operation as in stage 1, namely to involve as few people as possible.

Taking others with you may seem to be "ganging up" on the person.  However the others bear witness to the truth and the fact of the confrontation.

What might happen?  You may find the witnesses you try to take tell you that *you* are wrong, or they won't go with you.  Or you may discover something unexpected, which changes how you would view it.  For example, to use the illustration above, you confront your neighbour about not returning your lawnmower.  He responds: "Well, it's quite true that I asked for the lawnmower and then didn't return it to you. But don't you remember, it's *my* lawnmower! You borrowed it from me last year."

If you do not uncover anything unexpected like this, the approach will in all likelihood be successful. Expect success. If you get it, that's the end of the matter. Once you have resolved it, make sure that your one or two witnesses know it's resolved.

How many people should now be involved? The answer is only three or four, namely you, the other person, and your one or two witnesses.

## Stage 3: Inform the Church

You are unlikely to be here, although it's possible. We are now dealing with Matthew 18 verse 17, where it says, "Tell it to the church." What does this mean? It does *not* mean you should suddenly stand up in a worship time and blurt it out. Nor does it mean that you should begin to pass it around everyone you meet. Tell the leadership. They will decide if it's a genuine grievance, and if so will take it further (probably by repeating stages 1 and 2 at leadership level). If not, they will reprove *you*.

Only if there is still no response will it be brought before the whole Church, and even then *restoration* is what is in view, not revenge and not exposure. The matter has now escalated to the level of Church discipline, and is out of your hands.

The unfolding principle is: involve as few people as possible; but if it needs to be widened, for clarity it must become *general* so that everyone is told the same thing and has the same information.

Again, the further into this procedure we are, the less likely we are to be there. In the unlikely event of even this third approach being unsuccessful, serious action must be taken for the maintenance of a righteous testimony. This is the second part of verse 17. Even then, it's not a vengeful "kicking out", but still focused on restoration.

## Stage 4: Treat as an unbeliever

> *"...if he refuses to listen even to the church, treat him as you would a pagan or a tax collector."*    Matthew 18:17b

The word pagan, or Gentile as it's often translated, carries the sense of "not one of us". A tax collector was a Jew who had sold himself out to the occupying Roman forces to collect taxes for them from his fellow Jews.    It was understood that he lived off his overcharging.    They therefore viewed a tax collector as a turncoat and traitor.    Yet Jesus reached out to them and ate with them.    A summary phrase would seem to be "treat him as an unbeliever".

In 1 Corinthians 5 a situation is referenced where a member of the Church has committed serious sin and is apparently unrepentant. Paul's counsel is to put him out of the midst of the fellowship of the Church, also sombrely described as, "handing him over to Satan". This most serious form of church discipline is not vindictive, but is intended to lead to his restoration.

Entry to the church is by repentance.    Re-entry is also by repentance.    Once there is repentance, there can be full restoration *as a believer* and all will be well.

> *All Scripture is God-breathed and is useful for teaching,*
> *rebuking, correcting and training in righteousness*
> 2 Timothy 3:16

It can be difficult to follow through on discipline, and easier to buckle.    But if we deal with things according to God's Word, it will produce righteousness in the end.

The ideal is peace (see Romans 12:18; 14:19; Ephesians 4:3).    Yet since things *will* go wrong, we will sometimes need to operate the first approach described above, so we need to *know* it and *do* it.

As mentioned, this is a safety-factor teaching.    The aim is to walk in love.

> *If you really keep the royal law found in Scripture, "Love*
> *your neighbour as yourself," you are doing right.*
> James 2:8

> *Above all, love each other deeply, because love covers*
> *over a multitude of sins.*        *1 Peter 4:8*

> ⁴*Love is patient, love is kind.    It does not envy, it does*
> *not boast, it is not proud.    ⁵It is not rude, it is not self-*
> *seeking, it is not easily angered, it keeps no record of*
> *wrongs.    ⁶Love does not delight in evil but rejoices with*
> *the truth.    ⁷It always protects, always trusts, always*
> *hopes, always perseveres.*
> ⁸*Love never fails.    But where there are prophecies, they*
> *will cease; where there are tongues, they will be stilled;*

where there is knowledge, it will pass away.  *9*For we know in part and we prophesy in part, *10*but when perfection comes, the imperfect disappears.  *11*When I was a child, I talked like a child, I thought like a child, I reasoned like a child.  When I became a man, I put childish ways behind me.  *12*Now we see but a poor reflection as in a mirror; then we shall see face to face. Now I know in part; then I shall know fully, even as I am fully known.

*13*And now these three remain: faith, hope and love. But the greatest of these is love.    1 Corinthians 13:4-13

## Review Questions on Chapters 6 and 7

1. When someone wrongs us, and we get hurt or offended, we should: *(choose one)*

    A. Tell other people

    B. Tell no one but quietly seethe inside

    C. Look for a way to get our own back

    D. Forgive him

2. If someone does some bad thing to us, how does it compare to the things for which God has forgiven us? *(choose one)*

    A. It's probably worse

    B. It's probably about the same

    C. It could be worse or not so bad, it's impossible to say

    D. It's never as bad as the things God has forgiven us

3. If someone wrongs us, we forgive him, he does it again and repents again, how many times should we forgive him?    *(choose one)*

    A. 2 or 3 times

    B. Up to 7 times

    C. 490 times

    D. As often as necessary without counting how many times

4. If we refuse to forgive our fellow Christians, it may have a harmful effect on them.  TRUE or FALSE?

5. If we refuse to forgive our fellow Christians, it may have a harmful effect on ourselves.  TRUE or FALSE?

6. We should wait to forgive someone who wrongs us until he apologises.  TRUE or FALSE?

## Review Questions on Chapters 6 and 7 (continued)

7. First person: "I was wrong. Please forgive me."    Second person: "I've heard it all before. This time I'll wait and see if you really mean it before I forgive you."    Is this a correct response?

8. *"I don't feel able to forgive yet."*  Comment on this.

9. *"I'd like to forgive, but I can't."*    Comment on this.

10. When someone wrongs you, which of these reactions is correct?    *(choose one)*

    A. "Wait till I tell my friends what he did!"

    B. "I'd like to face him up with it but I haven't got the moral courage.   I think I'll write him a stinking letter."

    C. "I think I'll bounce it off my friend and maybe take him along with me for moral support."

    D. "I'm not looking forward to it, but I know I have to go to him and speak about it face to face."

11. If we need 2 or 3 witnesses, so we take 1 or 2 others, what is the unfolding principle?

12. The goal of all Church discipline is:    *(choose one)*

    A. Revenge

    B. Exposure

    C. Proper and just punishment for bad conduct

    D. Restoration

# EIGHT

# THE GRACE OF GIVING

**KEY VERSE:** But just as you excel in everything—in faith, in speech, in knowledge, in complete earnestness and in your love for us—see that you also excel in this grace of giving.          2 Corinthians 8:7

> *6Remember this: Whoever sows sparingly will also reap sparingly, and whoever sows generously will also reap generously. 7Each man should give what he has decided in his heart to give, not reluctantly or under compulsion, for God loves a cheerful giver. 8And God is able to make all grace abound to you, so that in all things at all times, having all that you need, you will abound in every good work.*
> *9As it is written:*
>
>> *"He has scattered abroad his gifts to the poor;*
>> *his righteousness endures forever."*
>
> *10Now he who supplies seed to the sower and bread for food will also supply and increase your store of seed and will enlarge the harvest of your righteousness. 11You will be made rich in every way so that you can be generous on every occasion, and through us your generosity will result in thanksgiving to God.*          2 Corinthians 9:6-11

## Ownership or Stewardship?

A man buys a house. Does he own it?

The question may seem ridiculous. We know that houses are bought and sold. But what about the land the house is built on? Was it the seller's to sell? In the beginning, *God* made the land, and He didn't sell it to anybody! It's *His*.

> *The earth is the Lord's and everything in it, the world and all who live in it*          Psalm 24:1

If when walking in a park a man found an expensive item, he'd say, "Whose is it?" Yet when we find ourselves, also valuable items, alive on planet Earth, we're unlikely to ask the same question.  We so often say, "It's *my* life!"  We should say, "Whose am I?"

Questions and considerations like this lead us to see that if we believe in and know God, we *own* nothing.  Everything we have is *His*, and we ourselves are His.  We're stewards of what we have, not owners.  And so when it comes to *giving* to God, the issue is not "*my* money."  It's already all His, and we're simply seeking to be faithful as good stewards.

## Biblical Giving Survey

The Old Testament understanding of giving was based on *tithes* (that is, one-tenth of our income or increase).  The understanding of offerings to God was:

*Offerings = Tithes + Free Will Offerings*

Tithes were *due*, and Free Will Offerings were offerings given by choice over and above the tithe.

In surveying the subject of giving in the Old Testament, we begin with the tithe, sometimes called the *first* tithe.  In the nation, there were twelve tribes, and one of these, the Levites, had no inheritance of land, and therefore no increase, or no income in our terms.  Their task was to be priests and to provide the tabernacle and temple services.  The other tribes were to tithe to the Lord, and the tithe was declared holy to the Lord (Leviticus 27:30).  The tithe was then given to the Levites for their livelihood (Numbers 18:21).  From this, the Levites tithed too, but that's another matter.

Other Scriptures speak of bringing the tithe to Jerusalem, and celebrating by eating some of it there in a feast.  There are two views, the first of which is that this represents a second ten per cent laid aside like a budgeting system so that individuals could participate in the big celebrations of the faith.  The other view is that this was the same tithe as previously discussed, but a little of it was eaten as celebration, and the remainder was for the Levites.  (See Deuteronomy 12:5-14 and 14:22-26.)  It seems that the Jews also struggled to interpret this, although by New Testament times we understand that they gave a tithe for the Levites *as well as* the tithe for the feast.  Therefore, we may be up to a giving level of 20% now!

Other Scriptures again refer to seemingly another tithe, sometimes called the "third" tithe, one taken up every three years (see Deuteronomy 14:28,29; 26:12-14).  This was collected and stored locally, and given to the Levites, the aliens, the fatherless, and the widows (the "landless") as a poor relief fund. Since this is generally considered as additional, we may now be up to a giving level of 23⅓%.

And then there was the Governmental Tithe. From the time of the kings, this was a tax tithe on the people to fund the King's court and government (see 1 Samuel 8:10-22 and 2 Kings 23:35). So we may now be as high as a giving level of 33⅓% (that is, one-third). If the "feast" tithe is the same as the first tithe, then the level is 23⅓%.

The Governmental tithe would correspond to income tax today, and so may the poor relief tithe every three years. The feast tithe, if it truly is separate, may fit still today in our budgeting, but if so, it's more personal.

But the basic tithe, that was holy to the Lord and was used for the support of the Levites and temple services, may still apply today, because we still have those who correspond to the Levites, namely the full-time Christian ministry. Paul wrote to the Corinthians:

> *Don't you know that those who work in the temple get their food from the temple, and those who serve at the altar share in what is offered on the altar? In the same way, the Lord has commanded that those who preach the gospel should receive their living from the gospel.*
> 1 Corinthians 9:13,14 (See 1 Corinthians 9:7-14)

For the Levites, it was by *birth*. For us it's by *gifting*. Those in the church recognised in this way are released from the need to be employed in order to give their full time to ministry.

But does the New Testament talk about tithing? There may be some hints, but there is only one clear reference, which is found in Matthew 23:23 (and its parallel in Luke 11:42). Here Jesus says to the Pharisees that they are so fastidious and pernickety that they are even tithing the increase in their herb garden, and yet are neglecting the more important matters of the Law—justice, mercy and faithfulness. His next statement is, "You should have practised the latter without neglecting the former." Stronger than it may at first appear, this is an endorsement of tithing, even of the herb garden!

That verse alone will be enough for some, but it may not be convincing for all. So what *does* the New Testament say about giving? It says we should give in the following ways:

| | |
|---|---|
| **Regularly** | 1 Corinthians 16:1,2 — Here it says weekly, on the first day of the week |
| **Willingly** | 2 Corinthians 8:3,12 — Not grudgingly giving as if under duress |
| **Generously** | 2 Corinthians 8:2; 9:5,11,13 |
| **Systematically** | 2 Corinthians 9:7a — First decide, and then follow through |
| **Cheerfully** | 2 Corinthians 9:7b — Not reluctantly or under compulsion, but joyously |
| **Proportionately** | 2 Corinthians 8:11-15; 9:6; 1 Corinthians 16:2 According to income and means |

On this last point, 2 Corinthians 9:6 speaks of sowing sparingly or generously, and this concept depends on proportionate giving. Jesus reckoned the widow who gave the two mites (Mark 12:41-44) more generous than those who gave much more. For her, what she gave was *everything*. For a millionaire, the same amount would have been virtually *nothing*. We can express and appreciate generosity only in proportionate terms.

The New Testament does not specifically say that the proportion should be 10%, but it does say that we should give a proportion.

Some take the view that the first members of the Church were so Jewish in their understanding, and therefore so tuned in to tithing already, that spelling it out was unnecessary. Others say that the New Testament makes no rule, or even that it deliberately makes no rule, and leaves it to the individual led by the Spirit.

Concerning fulfilling the Law, when Jesus said, for example, "You have heard that it was said, 'Love your neighbour and hate your enemy.' But I tell you: Love your enemies," what *He* said was a higher standard (Matthew 5:43,44). Thus perhaps in a New Testament "fulfilling" of tithing we should expect to give *at least* 10%. It's hard to see how we could settle for *less* than the Old Testament standard, and think it's *generous*.

> Our Liberty Church conclusion is that we should take the proportion as 10%, and so to tithe as the baseline in giving. It's not the Liberty *rule*, but it's the Liberty *recommendation*. Many have come to this same conclusion and can testify to the faithfulness of God in honouring it.

So the Old Testament understanding that Offerings = Tithes + Free Will Offerings is still basically true.

*Offerings = Baseline giving* (tithes, or other baseline giving) + *Free Will Offerings*

## The baseline: Tithes

Because the money is all His, the way to look at it is that it's not so much that we give God 10%, but rather that He gives us 90%.  And once we honour Him in this way, many will testify that the 90% seems to further than the 100% used to!   It is the experience of many that if we do not honour God by tithing, our money seems to fritter away.   But when we do, somehow there are no longer what appear to be holes in our wallets and purses.   The long-time Baptist pastor Dr W.A. Criswell told the story:

> I read the funniest thing: a man, a pastor was asked, "How many members do you have in your church?" He said, "I have 1,119 members."  And then the second question, "How many tithers do you have in your church?"   He said, "I have 1,119 tithers."  And the questioner was amazed, as I would be.  "What? You have 1,119 members and 1,119 tithers?  How could such a thing be?" He answered, "Well, about a hundred of them bring their tithes to the church, and God collects it from the rest of them."

Where do we bring the tithe?  Malachi 3:10 says, *"Bring the whole tithe into the storehouse".*  Most take this to mean the local church of which we're part.  Some people have had a different view, where they would give a tithe in total, but make a distribution of it, for example, some to missions, some to the Red Cross, some to a TV preacher, and some to the church.  We believe that this understanding is not optimal.   It is perfectly valid to give *offerings* to these other ministries, but the tithe is for the local church of which we're part. That's our contact point and our point of belonging to the wider church.  One implication of this is that the local church should give a portion of its income to support the wider work and ministry, and not simply use all its income for its own immediate benefit.

## Freewill giving: Offerings

Offerings are sacrificial. They represent money we *choose* to give above the baseline of tithes that we could perfectly validly spend on ourselves. Unlike tithes, offerings may be designated, for example for benevolence, or missions, or the building fund, and so on.

The old joke says, "When is a door not a door?" The answer is, "when it is ajar." Similarly, we could ask, "when is an offering not an offering?" This time the answer is, "when we don't tithe." Suppose you have a bill from Scottish Power for £150. You decline to pay the bill, but send them an offering of £30 as a "gift in appreciation". They would not accept the gift as a gift; rather they would deduct it from the £150 bill and calculate that you now owe them £120. In the same way, an offering is not an offering when you don't tithe.

## Seed and Bread

Some say, "All I want is enough to live on." That sounds pious and humble, but actually it's selfish! If all we have is enough to live on, we've nothing to give away. Returning to the passage 2 Corinthians 9:6-11, it speaks of abundance and enrichment, and yet the abundance is for *good works*, and the enrichment is for *generosity*. John Bunyan wrote:

> A man there was, though some did count him mad,
> The more he cast away, the more he had.

According to verse 10, God supplies two things, *seed* and *bread*. We sow seed and eat bread. In an ongoing way, we sow seed for a future and continuing harvest. But some of the seed we make into bread, and that sustains us in the here and now. Seed is for sowing and bread is for eating. That gives rise to two possible errors. The first is the error of eating your seed, where you consume what could and should be sown. The second is the error of sowing your bread. This is where you try to sow what you need to live on, like the mortgage money, for example. However, bread in the ground simply rots!

## Faith

All this sowing and reaping, all these tithes and offerings, represent a challenge, particularly for those to whom it's new. There's a *faith* dimension to it, a need to step out in faith. God invites us to test His faithfulness in this.  In fact, the matter of giving is the only place in the whole Bible where God invites us to *test* Him.

## Practical Matters

Proportionate giving (tithes, etc.) should be giving calculated on your *increase*, on what you earn or receive.  It should not be for example on student loans and most government benefits.  Very simply, if you have no earned income, then your earned income is zero, and 10% (or any proportion) of zero is zero.  Therefore you *do* tithe, and anything you can give is a free will offering.

If you are a UK taxpayer, under the Gift Aid scheme signing a simple form once will enable the church of which you're part to reclaim the tax you will have paid or will pay on your donations at no extra cost to you.  This adds extra (currently 25%) to the value of your actual donation.  However, to qualify for this, the church must be able to verify your giving.  Different local churches will handle this in different ways.  For Liberty Church, this means that your giving must be either by means of numbered envelopes (which are available on request) or by some kind of bank-related or online giving, including standing orders, internet and online banking, and cards. Information and forms for all these are available.

As mentioned above, the Bible speaks of weekly giving, in response to which most churches take up a weekly offering.  Those who are paid monthly (or four-weekly) will probably find it much easier to deal with tithing or other baseline giving monthly (or four-weekly), as the money comes.  However, even if you deal with your baseline giving monthly or by standing order, you can still participate in weekly giving by making a free will offering each week.

Whether you see it as completing your baseline giving, or adding a little extra, it seems that putting *something* in the offering basket each week, however small, can have a positive effect on your faith, and that of those around you.  But again, this is not a rule, simply a recommendation.

In giving offerings consisting of baseline proportionate giving (or tithes, as we understand it) together with free will offerings as outlined above, we are responding appropriately to God and His Word, and thereby taking proper responsibility for our part in supporting Liberty Church or the church of which we're part with our giving.

*And they did not do as we expected, but they gave themselves first to the Lord and then to us in keeping with God's will. ... But just as you excel in everything—in faith, in speech, in knowledge, in complete earnestness and in your love for us—see that you also excel in this grace of giving.*                    2 Corinthians 8:5,7

# NINE

# THE MATTER OF JUDGEMENT

This is a big subject with many Scriptures to consider. There is much more to say than we will say here. However the following notes and comments will serve our purpose.

## What happens when you die?

Most people have formed an opinion in response to this question, which means we have some ground to clear and some preconceptions to cut through in order to make a biblical response. Ultimately, our opinions don't matter, but only the truth of God's Word.

Jesus said: "I am the resurrection and the life. He who lives in me will live, even though he dies; and whoever lives and believes in me will never die." (John 11:25,26) The external body does die, but the inner person does *not*. To be away from the body is to be at home with the Lord — there is no "gap" in eternal life (2 Corinthians 5:6,8). We can be assured and confident for the future, even seeing death as gain (2 Corinthians 5:1,5,8; Philippians 1:21).

And one day, the inner person will be reunited with the body — a resurrection body, similar and yet at the same time very different, as was the case for Jesus. (See 1 Thessalonians 4:13-18 and 1 Corinthians 15:35-58.)

## What difference does this make right now?

As a believer, you have eternal life and the life is in the Son (1 John 5:11). You need not fear your own death. You can face death with confidence. (See Hebrews 2:14,15.) You can put your heart and soul into your work for the Lord — it's not in vain (1 Corinthians 15:58). Also you can be at peace about your loved ones who have died as believers. They have gone to be with the Lord and await their resurrection bodies. You will see them again and love them again. So be encouraged. No matter how bad the world may seem or may become, you can always have confidence (1 Thessalonians 5:9-11).

## Eternal judgement

There will be judgement when Jesus comes again.  Jesus will return as King (Acts 1:10,11; Titus 2:13).  Wisdom dictates that we not be overly concerned with *when*, but rather be ready *whenever*.

In the Bible, we see a *past* judgement, the judgement at the Cross. Here Satan was judged and his power over believers was broken. Here also the sins of the believer were judged and put away.  We also see several pictures of *future* judgement, of which we'll consider two: the *Great White Throne*, and the *Judgement Seat of Christ*.

## The Great White Throne

This is found in the book of Revelation, chapter 20:11-15

> *[11]Then I saw a great white throne and him who was seated on it.  Earth and sky fled from his presence, and there was no place for them.  [12]And I saw the dead, great and small, standing before the throne, and books were opened.  Another book was opened, which is the book of life.  The dead were judged according to what they had done as recorded in the books.  [13]The sea gave up the dead that were in it, and death and Hades gave up the dead that were in them, and each person was judged according to what he had done.  [14]Then death and Hades were thrown into the lake of fire.  The lake of fire is the second death.  [15]If anyone's name was not found written in the book of life, he was thrown into the lake of fire.*

In addition to the text, we can add the following comments:
- The wicked "die in their sins" (see John 8:24)
- Reference is made to "everlasting destruction" (see 2 Thessalonians 1:7-9
- Hell is described as a place of fire and of darkness (see Mark 9:43,48; Matthew 8:12)
- Jesus said more about hell than He said about heaven
- The "eternal fire" was not prepared for people (see Matthew 25:41)
- It doesn't make any difference to truth whether we *like* this or not or *believe* it or not.  But it should surely lead to some evangelistic fervour.

## The Judgement Seat of Christ

> *For we will all stand before God's judgement seat.  It is written: "As surely as I live,' says the Lord, 'every knee will bow before me; every tongue will confess to God.'" So then, each of us will give an account of himself to God.*
>
> Romans 14:10-12

> *For we must all appear before the judgement seat of Christ, that each one may receive what is due him for the things done while in the body, whether good or bad.*
>
> 2 Corinthians 5:10

This is the judgement of believers' works, motives and actions, but not sins, for rewards or non-rewards (see also 1 Corinthians 3:11-15). Because you are saved by grace through faith, you will not lose your salvation (Romans 8:1), but you may lose your reward.  As a believer, you will never be judged again to see whether you make it to heaven or not.  You will be judged to see whether your works on earth will stand the test of fire, leaving you something to offer Jesus.

In conclusion, we have nothing to fear as we continue in faith in Jesus Christ.  We can with confidence look forward to the future and even to death.  It will be better!

---

### Review Questions on *A Matter of Judgement*

1. What happens when a Christian dies?
2. Should Christians personally fear death?
3. When should you expect to get your "resurrection body"?
4. According to Revelation 20:15, who will ultimately be "thrown into the lake of fire"?
5. "The Bible says that God is love.  I don't think a loving God will throw anybody into hell."  Comment on this opinion.
6. Will believers be judged at the Great White Throne?
7. Will believers be judged at the Judgement Seat of Christ?
8. *What* is judged at the Judgement Seat of Christ?
9. When are the sins of believers judged?
10. In the light of the Great White Throne Judgement for unbelievers, what should our attitude be towards those who are without Christ?

# TEN

# THE CHURCH:

# LEADERSHIP AND STRUCTURE

In a well-known passage of Scripture, Jesus said, "...on this rock I will build my church, and the gates of Hades will not overcome it" (Matthew 16:18). Much has been made of this verse, but it is clear that the Church the gates of Hades will not overcome is the Church *Jesus* is building! We cannot therefore simply choose to build the church any way we fancy. We must be obedient to the way *Jesus* does it.

There are many expressions of the church, some very different from others. No doubt some of these may be spurious, yet it seems that Jesus is the Builder of variety! The various expressions of the church are responsible for their own obedience to the Builder. The question for *us* is: How do things happen in a church like ours?

In Chapter 3, we looked at three pictures of the church in the context of relationships. Now in the context of structure, here are three more pictures of the church.

## The Church as a spiritual army

Several Scriptures give us the picture of the Church as the Army of God, in the conflict of the ages. Wearing the full armour of God, we are soldiers in the army, enduring hardship, taking orders, seeking to please our commanding officer, with Jesus Himself as the Captain of our Salvation. In the army, discipline is necessary. So too is an awareness of the chain of command, and submission to authority (see Matthew 8:9).

## The Church as the spiritual nation

The Bible pictures the Church as the people of God, God's holy nation (see 1 Peter 2:9,10).  As in any nation, structure and government are important.

## The Church as a spiritual flock

The picture is developed in John's gospel, chapter 10.  We are God's sheep, and Jesus is the Shepherd.  But there are also under-shepherds, who oversee the local flock.

All three of these pictures demonstrate the need for organisation and structure.   How then is a church like ours organised and structured?

First, the Church is not a democracy.   Democracy means the people rule, and that's not the way for the Church.  Let's be quick to note that the Church is not a dictatorship either!   The Church is intended to be a theocracy, meaning that *God* rules.  God's rule in the Church is exercised through delegated authority, that is, recognised local leadership.   One of the reasons people join one local church rather than another is that they recognise the authority of God in its leadership.

In the book of Exodus, when Moses was wearing out himself and the people by trying to do everything, his father-in-law Jethro gave him some wise counsel (see Exodus 18:13-26).   He told Moses to appoint men over thousands, hundreds, fifties and tens, and train them to handle the straightforward matters.  The more complicated matters could be passed on, ultimately to Moses himself.   Moses adopted this model of delegated structure, and a similar model is very effective in the pastoral organisation of the Church.   Every member may be in a small group (in Liberty Church called a Life Group), which is the first line of pastoral care.   In addition, there are *Elders* and *Pastor(s)*.

Trustees assist the Elders in attending to the financial and business aspects of the Church.  As for most UK churches, Liberty Church is a charity, and the Trustees are responsible for the governance of the Church as a charity.

Although this is structured, it does not represent a conventional hierarchy.   All believers in a Church are equally important and of equal value to God, and are equally loved by God.   Yet we have different giftings, roles and functions.   The gifting, role and function of some includes leadership and government.   The principle of leadership is not some lording it over the rest, but leadership through servanthood. (See Mark 10:42-45 and 1 Peter 5:1-4.)

Leadership is God's way of doing things.  It's often been said, "God so loved the world that He didn't send a committee."  God appoints leadership in the Church.  The existing leaders recognise those whom God has appointed, and commission them.  That's the way it works. Although someone may be appointed to a leadership position by human beings, that doesn't automatically make him a true leader. The "trick" is to discern those whom God is appointing, and put *them* in leadership positions.

There are three categories of church leaders, but *a leader will often be in more than one category*.  Here we'll call them:

1.  Ephesians 4 Ministries
2.  Pastors and Elders
3.  Supporting Leaders

and look at them one by one.

## First category: Ephesians 4 Ministries

This category is also known by some other names.  It is sometimes termed *Ascension Ministries*, and sometimes simply *Ministries*.  Some refer to those concerned as *Ministers* or *Fivefold Ministers*.  The problem in terminology is that we use the words *ministry* and *minister* (which really mean *service* and *servant* respectively) in so many different ways, with subtly different meanings.  It is even more confusing in Scotland, where the Church of Scotland uses *Minister* as a title for one of its fulltime church leaders, often called *Pastor* elsewhere.  However, we have to call them something.  *Ephesians 4 Ministries* is used here because the scriptural basis for the category is found in the very important Ephesians chapter 4:

> *⁷But to each one of us grace has been given as Christ apportioned it. ⁸This is why it says:*
>
> *"When he ascended on high,*
> *he led captives in his train*
> *and gave gifts to men."*
>
> *⁹(What does "he ascended" mean except that he also descended to the lower, earthly regions? ¹⁰He who descended is the very one who ascended higher than all*

> *the heavens, in order to fill the whole universe.) [11]It was he who gave some to be apostles, some to be prophets, some to be evangelists, and some to be pastors and teachers, [12]to prepare God's people for works of service, so that the body of Christ may be built up [13]until we all reach unity in the faith and in the knowledge of the Son of God and become mature, attaining to the whole measure of the fullness of Christ.*        Ephesians 4:7-13

There are five in the list: Apostles, Prophets, Evangelists, Shepherds, and Teachers.   Some translations, including the one above, say "pastors" rather than "shepherds", but the word is *shepherds* and is translated as such everywhere else it occurs.  We will use the word *shepherds* in this sense, and reserve the word *pastors* for the sense of the second category below, thus avoiding some confusion.

The important thing to see is that these five are not just people who have gifts, but rather they are *gifts of people* from Jesus to His Church.  All of us benefit from these gifts to the Body of Christ.  Their purpose and effect is to "prepare God's people" (or to "equip the saints") for "works of service" (or for "the work of the ministry"), so that the Body of Christ may be built up.

These Ephesians 4 Ministries are recognised by their gift and function.  They do not hold a *position* in the *local* church, unless they are in another leadership category in addition.  They will be based in a local church somewhere, but they are gifts to the wider church, and generally will be recognised by other local churches also.  Every local church will benefit from the input of these Ministries, who will help promote a balanced and full-orbed Church (see Ephesians 4:11-16).

## Second category: Pastors and Elders

Elders, also called Overseers, shepherd and oversee the local Church.  They *do* hold a position or office in the local Church.

The title "pastor" is used in various ways. It is often used to distinguish a vocational elder from the other elders, and/or to identify the lead elder.  Fairly commonly, a pastor will be an Ephesians 4 ministry in addition.  If so, he will not necessarily be a *shepherd* in the Ephesians 4 sense; he may be for example an *evangelist* or a *teacher*.  However it is perfectly possible that he will not be an Ephesians 4 ministry at all.  Indeed, this possibility is quite likely if there are several pastors in a local church, for example a youth pastor or a children's pastor or a worship pastor.

Pastors and Elders exercise a *securing* leadership function as they shepherd, oversee and rule the local Church.    Please note the following passages: Acts 20:28-31; 1 Peter 5:1-4; 1 Timothy 5:17-20; 1 Thessalonians 5:12,13; Hebrews 13:17.

## Third category: Supporting Leaders

This is likely to be a diverse category.    They may be ministry heads, team leaders, small group leaders, coordinators, administrators and so on.    Examples would include: Children's Ministry Leader; Set-Up Coordinator; Life Group Leader; Trustee; and others.    Again, some of these may be in other categories in addition.

Some Supporting Leaders will in scriptural terms be Deacons, whether or not they have that title.    (See 1 Timothy 3; Philippians 1:1.)

## Some additional characteristics of a church like ours

What other hallmarks may characterise a church like ours?    We can answer that question in a number of areas, first of all in our view of the Bible.    We believe that God's revelation in the Bible is more important than the traditions and heritage of our local church.    We fully acknowledge that we do have traditions.    However, if we become convinced that our traditions and practices are out of line with the Bible, we change.

Additionally, we believe that the record of the interaction with God that we see in the New Testament gives us the pattern for what we should expect today.    This has wide application, but includes the areas of spiritual gifts and supernatural ministry.

Secondly, our expectation is that God is near rather than far.    We believe that although God is Almighty, is the Creator of the whole universe and lives in unapproachable light, yet He is knowable and wants to be intimate with us, speak to us, and lead us day to day. The emphasis is on stressing the reality of a relationship with God, rather than a distant religion.    We believe that God is not remote from us, and His Presence may be experienced.    Accordingly, worship is not simply *in praise of God*, but is actually interacting with the Holy Spirit of God—that we may meet God and know His Presence in worship.

Thirdly, we see that the Church is not the same as or limited to the meetings.  We see Christianity not as a weekly or twice-weekly activity, but as life and lifestyle.  We stress relationships and fellowship, living out the "one anothers" of the New Testament (see the list on page 23).

Finally, we understand that we exist for a purpose beyond ourselves.  We are aware of a sense of mission, having been *sent* by God to those outside the church.  Along with the rest of God's people, we're on a mission as His agents to the world.  This does not mean that we neglect the care of one another, but it does mean that our purpose does not end there.  Jesus said:

> *"Therefore go and make disciples of all nations, baptising them in the name of the Father and of the Son and of the Holy Spirit, and teaching them to obey everything I have commanded you.  And surely I am with you always, to the very end of the age."*
>
> Matthew 28:19,20

# ELEVEN

# FAITH

Faith is important, a critical issue for us. God says in Isaiah, *"If you do not stand firm in your faith, you will not stand at all."* (Isaiah 7:9) *"We walk by faith, not by sight."* (2 Corinthians 5:7) *"And without faith it is impossible to please God."* (Hebrews 11:6)

Moreover, our *understanding* of faith is a critical issue. So many of the promises in the New Testament are expressed in terms of faith; and so many Christians do not live in the good of them, for reasons connected with faith.

We begin with a biblical definition, drawn from Hebrews 11:1. Here it is in various versions:

> *Now faith is being sure of what we hope for and certain of what we do not see.*                    NIV

> *Now faith is the assurance of things hoped for, the conviction of things not seen.*            NAS/ESV

> *Now faith is the substance of things hoped for, the evidence of things not seen.*                    KJV

> *Now faith is the assurance (the confirmation, the title-deed) of things [we] hope for, being the proof of things [we] do not see and the conviction of their reality—faith perceiving as real fact what is not revealed to the senses.*
>
>                                        AMP

Thus faith is not nebulous and airy-fairy—a floating, intangible concept—but rather it is *substance*, therefore something substantial.

## The difference between faith and hope

Hope is essential. You cannot live life without hope. The Bible says that hope deferred makes the heart sick. If that's what hope *deferred* does, hope that's *lost* is even worse. To have no hope is literally to be *desperate* — it's what the word means. Further, hope is foundational. Notice from the Hebrews 11:1 definition above that *faith* rests on *hope*.    Yet for all the value of hope, and all its undergirding of faith, faith and hope are not the same thing.

We normally use the word hope as an expression of wishful thinking.    Someone invites us to an event, and we say, "I'd like to be there, but I'm not sure I can.    I *hope* to be there."    Biblical hope is something stronger than that.    Biblical hope may be described as *a confident expectation of a future event*.    That sounds like *faith* to many people.

The New Testament depicts the Second Coming of Jesus, a future event, in the words: *"...while we wait for the blessed hope—the glorious appearing of our great God and Saviour, Jesus Christ"* (Titus 2:13).    It's not that we're in doubt or uncertainty about it.    We're confident in the expectation.    Yet it's called our *blessed hope* rather than our blessed *faith* because it's *future*.    Hope is a confident expectation of a future event.

Many years ago I learned Colin Urquhart's definitions of faith and hope and have used them ever since.    He put it this way:

> *"Hope is believing you will have what you don't see; faith is believing you already have what you don't see."*

In both cases, you are believing something; and in both cases you don't *see* it.    The difference is that hope is *future* and faith is *now*.

Why is this important?    The implications are clear.    Consider the case of healing.    Jesus told some people, "Your faith has healed you."    He did *not* say, "Your *hope* has healed you."    Someone may ask a sick person, "Do you believe God will heal you?" and the person may answer, "Yes, I believe God will heal me."    That may sound like faith.    But in reality it's only hope—a confident expectation of a future event.    Faith would say, "I believe God has healed me."

Now this sounds very confusing, as if we're trying to pretend.    We may protest, "If it's happened, wouldn't I *know*?"    We may know *by faith*, but perhaps not yet *by sight*.    That's the language of faith.    Jesus said:

> *"Therefore I tell you, whatever you ask for in prayer, believe that you have received it, and it will be yours."*
>
> Mark 11:24

It's as you believe you have received it—that it's in your pocket as it were, although you can't pull it out and see it or prove it to anyone—that it *will* be visibly and demonstrably yours.

> Now faith is the substance of things hoped for, the evidence of things not seen.                    Hebrews 11:1 KJV

To use an illustration from Colin Urquhart, some prayers are answered like rockets and some like tortoises. Sometimes the answer to prayer is immediately apparent. These are the rockets, and we like those times. At other times however it's not quite so clear. When we pray, we may picture it as a tortoise being sent from heaven, a tortoise that is both the answer and that brings the answer. It moves slowly, but it's coming. In the language of Mark 11:24, we believe we have received it—it's been granted, the tortoise is on its way. We can therefore thank God by *faith*, and as we continue in faith, the second part of the verse says that it will be ours—the tortoise will arrive, and we can then thank God by *sight*. But the problem is that we become impatient, or we think it's not working, so we stop believing the promise. In the picture, it's then as if the tortoise stops; and it won't start moving again until we click back into faith.

To follow through on the case of healing, we pray, and then confess, "I believe God has healed me." We *believe we have received it*—not so much the healing as the answer, the tortoise is on its way— *and it will be ours*. As we continue in faith, and thanking God by faith, maintaining our confession, the time will come when the healing will be apparent, and we can thank God also by sight.

Perhaps we think, "Well if that's faith, I'm not sure I'm *ever* in faith!" However, consider salvation. As believers in Jesus, we believe we are saved. We can't *prove* it, but we *believe* it *now*. The time will come when that salvation will be clearly visible. In the meantime, again using Mark 11:24, we believe we have received it and it will be ours. Therefore we *are* in faith for our salvation.

## Faith comes

The Bible tells us:

> So faith comes by hearing, and hearing by the word of Christ.                    Romans 10:17

Every good gift comes from God (see James 1:17). Faith *comes*, and specifically comes by hearing the word of Christ. Dr Larry Lea defined faith in this way: "Faith is the inner knowledge that God's Word has been applied to my life."

There's an interesting story told in Mark 9:14-27. It concerns a father trying to get help for his son who suffers from seizures. The father had brought him to Jesus, but Jesus was away at that time with some of His disciples. The other disciples tried to help, but all that happened was that it drew attention to the problem. Then Jesus returned. When the demon in the boy saw Jesus, it threw the boy into a customary convulsion. As Jesus dialogued with the boy's father, the father said, "If you can do anything, take pity on us and help us." Jesus replied, "'If you can'? Everything is possible for him who believes." Then the father exclaimed, "I do believe; help me overcome my unbelief!" Apparently at that moment and at the word of Christ, *faith* came.

My friend was selling his house. The uptake was slow, and he asked some people to pray for a sale. I did, and a moment came when I quite naturally switched in prayer from *asking* God to do it to *thanking* God for doing it. That, I think, is the moment when faith came—*believe that you have received it and it will be yours*. The house sold a short time afterwards.

The believer has a problem, and turns to the Bible. As he reads, a relevant passage seems to be highlighted, then another. As a result, *faith* comes. That's often how it works.

## Faith obeys

The fear of presumption leads to fatalism—we don't want to get it wrong, so we'll just wait and see. But faith *acts*, and specifically faith obeys.

The only way forward is across the ravine. It's too wide to jump, and the only possibility seems to be a rickety old plank acting as a bridge. Faith is not standing on the edge wondering, "If I step out on that plank, will it take my weight?" Faith is not standing on the edge being absolutely convinced that if I stepped out on the plank, it would take my weight. Faith is stepping out on the plank.

David Pawson used to tell the story of a game he would play with his children when they were very young. He would stand at the foot of the staircase, and one of them would climb up to the third or fourth step. He would say, "Jump", the child would jump, and he would catch him. The game was called "Faith". Faith is not standing on the step wondering, "If I jump, will Daddy catch me?" Faith is not standing on the step being absolutely convinced that if I jump, Daddy will catch me.   Once he says "Jump", faith is jumping and trusting Daddy.

Faith must be completed by obedience.   In John chapter 4, the royal official's son lay sick at Capernaum.   Having heard that Jesus had arrived in Cana, the official went in search of Him to beg Him to come and heal his son, who was close to death.   Jesus said, "You may go. Your son will live."   Faith came, but now he had a dilemma.   He'd just made the journey of over twenty miles.   Having risked leaving his son to look for Jesus, he'd found Jesus.   But now this one in whom was his only hope was saying to go back and his son would live.   Should he obey, leaving the one in whom was his hope?   Or should he try to get Him to come too?   The man took Jesus at His word and departed.   On the long journey back, his servants met him with the news that his son had recovered, at what proved to be the exact hour that Jesus had said, "Your son will live."   Faith must be completed by obedience.

In a well-known story, it was dark and there was a storm on the Sea of Galilee.   The disciples of Jesus were out in a boat labouring at the oars.   Jesus went out to them walking on the water.   The terrified disciples thought He was a ghost, but Jesus reassured them.   Then Peter said, "Lord, if it's you, tell me to come to you on the water."   Jesus answered only one word: "Come."   That was the word of Christ to Peter, and faith came.   But Peter had to decide if he was going to obey or disobey.   He obeyed, and walked on water.   Or perhaps we could say that he walked by faith on the word of Christ to him.

## Faith grows

Let's return to the story of the boy who had seizures, but this time from Matthew's gospel.   Jesus rebuked the demon.   It came out of the boy and he was healed (see Matthew 17:18).   Later the disciples asked Jesus why they were unable to drive it out, and in reply He said:

> *"Because you have so little faith.   I tell you the truth, if you have faith as small as a mustard seed, you can say to this mountain, 'Move from here to there' and it will move. Nothing will be impossible for you."*    Matthew 17:20 NIV

The answer sounds confusing.  Most of us feel like we've got mustard-seed-sized faith, but we haven't moved any mountains recently!  And if mustard-seed-sized faith can move mountains, who wants or needs any more?  Are we missing something?

If we look at the words of Jesus' answer more literally, something helpful emerges.  The words "as small" are not really there in the original, but are added by the translators to help us understand what they think is the meaning.  It actually says, *"... if you have faith as a mustard seed, you can say ...".*  Then if we compare Matthew 13:31,32, we find:

> *"... [The mustard seed] is the smallest of all your seeds, yet when it grows, it is the largest of garden plants and becomes a tree, so that the birds of the air come and perch in its branches."*                    Matthew 13:32

The implication is that "faith as a mustard seed" could refer to *growing* faith.  It may start small, but not stay that way.

How does our faith grow?  Here are five possible answers.  First, faith is a fruit of the Spirit, where we bear what the Spirit produces in and through us.  (See Galatians 5:22,23.  Many translations say "faithfulness" but the word is "faith".)  Secondly, through praying in the Holy Spirit (see Jude 20).  Thirdly, through praying and believing while we're praying.  Fourthly, through meditating on the Word of God.  Fifthly, through being immediately obedient to the promptings of the Holy Spirit.

Seeing prayer answered builds faith.  It's not so much a question of how *much* faith you have, but your capacity to believe God.  Thinking back to the child's game, you can jump with greater confidence from where you've jumped before, and may even be able to stretch higher, but for all that, the jumping is still by faith.  Association with others can also help.  Being around people of faith can build your faith.  Conversely, being around some other people can weaken your faith.

It's a big subject, and it seems that there's always more to learn about faith.  In summary however: hope is future and faith is now; faith comes; faith obeys; faith grows.

## Review Questions on Chapter 11

1. What's the only way we can get God's favour (grace)?

2. What is Dr Larry Lea's definition of faith?

3. *"At some future time, Jesus will come again."*    Is this FAITH or HOPE, using Biblical meanings?

4. According to Colin Urquhart's definition, what is HOPE?

5. According to Colin Urquhart's definition, what is FAITH?

6. Romans 10:17   *"Faith comes by hearing and hearing by"* what?

7. Faith is a feeling.  TRUE or FALSE?

8. *"I'm not sure if it's God's will to heal her, but I believe He can—He can do anything!—and if He wants to, He will."* Is this faith?   YES or NO

9. *"I think what I'll do is resign my job and step out in faith believing God to support me somehow."*    Is this more likely to be faith or presumption?

10. *"Faith must be completed by"* what?

11. *"It's not so much a question of how MUCH faith you have, but your"* what?

# TWELVE

# WHERE DO WE GO FROM HERE?

Take a word out of context and you can change or lose its meaning. Put it in to context and the meaning becomes clear. Our lives are like that. Out of context we can become confused or errant. In context, our meaning and purpose become clear.

The context for our personal purpose in God is the purpose of the *Church*. And the context for the Church is the eternal purpose of *God*, expressed in this way:

> *... to bring all things in heaven and on earth together under one Head, even Christ.*          Ephesians 1:10

That's the context, and that's where we go in our thinking when the questions of personal purpose come—and they do come.

"What's the point of life?" "Why am I here?" "What's it all about?"

We often hear such questions asked, sometimes in honest searching, sometimes in frustration. Followers of Jesus, who know that they are part of the Church, the Body of Christ, have the answers.

> *Instead, speaking the truth in love, we will in all things grow up into him who is the Head, that is, Christ. From him the whole body, joined and held together by every supporting ligament, grows and builds itself up in love, as each part does its work.*          Ephesians 4:15,16

We know in an overall sense what it's all about, and we are motivated to play our part. And yet we are still left wondering, "What *is* my part? What's the work that *I* am supposed to do? Where do I go from here?"

## Purpose

There are great benefits of a sense of purpose. Purpose gives *focus*. It means that we're looking at what we're going for. Purpose brings *meaning*. We have a reason to bother now—it *matters*.

Purpose leads to *fulfilment*.   We're fulfilled by doing the things designed and prepared for us to do.

On the other hand, without a sense of purpose we can drift through our days in fruitlessness, playing out ineffective and unproductive lives.  Without purpose, we can relate to the feeling of Ecclesiastes—"Meaningless, meaningless, everything is meaningless!"  We may be busy doing things, but they are not necessarily the *right* things.  They may not be *bad* things, but how would we know if they are right?  They are things we stumble into, without fulfilment.

Fire extinguishers serve a useful purpose, and self-closing fire doors serve a useful purpose.   But how often do we see fire extinguishers propping open fire doors?   That's something neither was designed for, and it undermines their proper function.

In our young days, my brother and I shared a bedroom, and a day came when we got new beds.  These were unlike the old-style beds we were used to—these were *divans*, where the mattress rested on a low base, which had four dumpy screw-in legs, one at each corner.  Being younger, my brother had a habit of jumping on his bed, and did so to such an extent that one of the dumpy screw-in legs buckled and broke off.  For years afterwards, his bed was held up by three dumpy screw-in legs and a pile of books!

The books in the pile were doing *something*, something useful.  They were fulfilling a role they had stumbled into.  But it was not the purpose for which they were *designed*.   Books are designed to be read.  We can be like that.  Some of us spend our time faithfully holding up beds, as it were—but that's *leg* work, not *our* work.

Perhaps we are simply drifting, drifting to a place of numbness in the unresolved conflict between conscience and lifestyle, and spinning our wheels.

It doesn't need to be that way.   We can *serve* God's purpose. Jesus on earth had great purpose, and He modelled purposeful living for us.  God has a purpose in general, but also a purpose for each of us.   We can seek to *serve* God's purpose, both in general and in terms of our unique part.

Acts 13:36 tells us: *"For when David had served God's purpose in his own generation, he fell asleep; he was buried with his fathers".*  That would give rise to a good epitaph: "He served God's purpose in his generation."  For us, it would be a good goal.  Several years ago, Mark Altrogge turned it into a song:

*I want to serve the purpose of God in my generation;*
*I want to serve the purpose of God while I am alive.*
*I want to give my life for something that will last forever;*
*Oh, I delight, I delight to do Your will.*
*What is on Your heart? Tell me what to do.*
*Let me know Your will and I will follow You.*

How do we serve God's purpose in Liberty Church?

## Liberty Church

Liberty Church has a vision

*Our vision is for a family of believers, committed to God and to each other, where people of all ages are finding hope, coming to faith and growing in their relationship with God as we follow Christ together.*

Liberty Church has five purpose statements:

1. Worship—Liberty Church exists to worship and glorify God.
2. Family—Liberty Church exists to be a strong, loving family of God's people.
3. Equipping—Liberty Church exists to equip and encourage people as they follow Jesus.
4. Outreach—Liberty Church exists to communicate the Good News of Jesus through words and actions.
5. Mission—Liberty Church exists to partner with God in His mission to the world.

In addition, Liberty Church has certain values, things we hold in an ongoing way that shape our approach to fulfilling our vision and purpose. Here are some:

1. We value personal relationship with God, through faith in Christ.
2. We value personal and intentional growth to spiritual maturity in the grace of God.
3. We value prayer as a two-way conversation with God, which nurtures our relationship with Him.
4. We value the Bible as the written word of God to us, the heart and foundation of our teaching and equipping. The message of the Bible is timeless and

true for every generation and should be communicated in a culturally relevant manner.

5. We value the church meeting together regularly as one body and in small groups for worship, prayer, equipping and fellowship.
6. We value the presence and power of God seen in signs, wonders, healing, miracles, and gifts of the Holy Spirit, glorifying Jesus and building His Church.
7. We value the Church as the body of Christ, one body with many individually and uniquely gifted parts which builds itself up in love as each part does its work.
8. We value all people as uniquely made in the image of God and loved by Him, endeavouring to treat every person with acceptance, respect, dignity and significance.
9. We value Jesus' commission to the Church to go into all the world and make disciples of all nations.

Our vision, purpose and values are based on our beliefs. Our Statement of Beliefs may be found on page 89.

## Getting into service

We serve in accordance with gifting, calling and vision. It's not a case of the next available person meeting the next urgent need. Yet the way to *discover* gifting or *assess* calling and vision is to start to serve *somewhere*. People often find joy and gifting serving in an unexpected area.

Clearly, there are some aspects of ministry that *must* happen, creating vacancies to be filled. But in most cases we believe that gifting, calling and vision should determine organised ministry, and not the other way round. This avoids square pegs in round holes.

In the experience of the church, it's common for someone to serve in a valued role for a long time, and then when he or she lays down the ministry, or is no longer able to continue, we look for a replacement. However, we don't have anyone who fits that exact shape of hole; so we force in the least unlikely peg. But it doesn't work. It's not a fit. At times like that, we need to remember that the ministry role was probably designed in the beginning to suit the person. Now that the person can't continue, that particular ministry position should probably close.  New positions are begun to suit the "shape" of the present "pegs".

Again, in a practical discovery sense, we may not know what shape of peg we are.  We can't find out by looking in the mirror!  We have to get moving by trying *something*.  Begin to serve where there is a need or an opportunity, and allow God to direct us in motion.

On a tour of the Cape Canaveral launch site, the tour guide noted that the guidance system for the rockets is handled by mission control in Houston, and doesn't kick in until the rocket reaches a certain height.  Someone asked without thinking, "Why is that?"  The tour guide tersely replied, "A rocket on a launch pad doesn't need guidance!"  We first get moving, and then God's guidance can kick in.

Of course, not every ministry position is available on a volunteer basis!  But some positions *are*.  There are some things we *always* need, and there's probably a task you can begin to do immediately. In terms of involvement with people, there are Life Groups to join. And everyone can start to serve by giving financially.

## A sense of destiny

A key text is found in Ephesians 2:10

> For we are all God's workmanship, created in Christ Jesus to do good works, which God prepared in advance for us to do.

We are God's workmanship, "fearfully and wonderfully made" (see Psalm 139:14).  We are created for good works, and equipped to do them.

How is He leading you?  What do you want to do?  God may give you a vision, or draw you to a particular area of ministry or outreach. He may show you something to join or something to develop.  You're on an adventure in God.  The adventure has begun, and even now it continues.

Where do you go from here?

## Liberty Church Statement of Belief

The following statements are fundamental truths that together form a basis of what we believe.

1. We believe in one God eternally existing in three persons: The Father, the Son and the Holy Spirit.

2. We believe in the sovereignty and grace of God the Father, God the Son and God the Holy Spirit in creation, providence, revelation, redemption and final judgement.

3. We believe in the divine inspiration of the whole Bible and its entire trustworthiness and supreme authority in all matters of faith and conduct.

4. We believe in the incarnation of God's eternal Son, the Lord Jesus Christ, at the same time fully divine and fully human. We believe in His virgin birth, His sinless life, His substitutionary death, His bodily resurrection and His glorious exaltation.

5. We believe that God created man in His own image, but that mankind was corrupted by sin, making him subject to God's wrath and condemnation; and that now in his natural state, man is a sinner, lost, without hope and without God.

6. We believe in the substitutionary atonement of Jesus Christ as the sole and all-sufficient ground of redemption from the guilt and power of sin, and from its eternal consequences.

7. We believe in the justification of the sinner by God's grace through faith alone.

8. We believe that the Gospel, the good news of all that God has done for us in Jesus Christ for our redemption, is the power of God for the salvation of everyone who believes. We further believe that the Church is committed by the command of Christ to the proclamation of the Gospel throughout the world.

9. We believe that those who respond to the Gospel message with repentance and saving faith are regenerate, justified and free from condemnation. We believe that this salvation is entirely the gift of God by grace through faith, and is not by works or human merit.

10. We believe in the illuminating, regenerating, indwelling and sanctifying work of God the Holy Spirit. We further believe that the power and gifts of the Holy Spirit are available to believers today.

11. We believe that all followers of Jesus form the universal Church, the Body of which Christ is the Head. As part of this universal Church, we further believe that the local Church exists for the purposes of worship, fellowship, outreach, equipping, and mission.

12. We believe in the personal, visible return of the Lord Jesus Christ in power and glory to consummate His Kingdom and to judge the world.